"Get off my property," she screamed. "Get off, or I'll shoot."

Chills shot up my spine as my hand slowly loosened on the weathered gatepost and I turned to face the shrill voice behind me. "The Lady," our euphemism for the neighbor across the street, stood with her feet firmly apart and the devil in her eyes. "Do you want to get shot?" she bellowed menacingly. "Now git!"

Although I was sure it was not her property, as we held the deed to it, I walked over to where she was planted to try and straighten out the matter. I figured it was just another of her harassments, but I held no illusions that she would hesitate to use the gun. With a girl in juvenile hall, another just released from the county jail, and the boy involved in a recent assault with a deadly weapon, her family was not known for its love and peace.

"I own that property you were standin' on, and I don't want no trespassin'!" she said defiantly, cocking her head to one side and raising her nose a little higher in the air. "No, sir, just stay off."

TRIAL BY DEATH & FIRE

D. Carl Anderson

Review and Herald Publishing Association
Nashville, TN   Washington, DC

Copyright © 1980 by
Review and Herald Publishing Association
Published in Nashville, Tennessee

This book was
Edited by Gerald Wheeler
Designed by Mark O'Connor

Type set: 11/12 Palatino
Printed in U.S.A.

Library of Congress Cataloging in Publication Data

Anderson, D   Carl, 1939-
  Trial by death and fire.

  1. Mr. A's Boys' Ranch. 2. Church work with problem children. 3. Anderson, D. Carl, 1939-   I. Title.

BV4464.A52   362.7'4'0979441   80-14446
ISBN 0-8127-0292-1

Contents

Do It Now	7
Little Dividends	17
Wandering in the Wilderness	24
Deadline Decisions	30
"Blackerry Jam"	37
"Where Your Treasure Is . . ."	41
In Spite of Us	49
The "Piece" Makers	56
A Cornhuskin' or a Hangin'	62
Triumph or Defeat	72
The Lead That Finally Led	78
Fire in the Night	90
Safe in a Boxcar	99
Blessings Always Boomerang	108
Death Gives Way to Victory	118
"Give, . . . and It Shall Be Given"	124
Help!	133
Joy and Grief	143
It's a Boys' World	151

Chapter 1

Do It Now

"Get off my property," she screamed. "Get off, or I'll shoot."

Chills shot up my spine as my hand slowly loosened on the weathered gatepost and I turned to face the shrill voice behind me. "The Lady," our euphemism for the neighbor across the street, stood with her feet firmly apart and the devil in her eyes. "Do you want to get shot?" she bellowed menacingly. "Now git!"

Although I was sure it was not her property, as we held the deed to it, I walked over to where she was planted to try and straighten out the matter. I figured it was just another one of her harassments, but I held no illusions that she would hesitate to use the gun. With a girl in juvenile hall, another just released from the county jail, and the boy involved in a recent assault with a deadly weapon, her family was not known for its love and peace.

"I own that property you were standin' on, and I don't want no trespassin'!" she said defiantly, cocking her head to one side and raising her nose a little higher in the air. "No, sir, just stay off."

Carefully I explained to her that we had purchased the property and had the deed to it.

"Nope," she said, "you don't. Your deed only goes to that old road, so you're crossin' ten feet of my land, and I won't have you doin' it."

"What could happen next?" I thought to myself.

I told her that I would go down to the courthouse to check it out. As I started to get into the car, she continued. "Let me just give you a little advice. We don't want them kids here, and we never will. Just yesterday I was talkin' to another neighbor, and he says that if your group is somehow able to 'con' that planning board into lettin' you come, you still won't be stayin' 'cause there would be an accidental fire started over there, and you'd be burned out. And maybe some of them kids would even be hurt!"

It was not exactly the type of hospitality one would expect in a place named Welcome Valley, and not until later did we begin to understand why.

The rest of the day I spent tracing down the property lines, discovering that she was partially right—we didn't own that strip of land. But neither did she! We had, indeed, purchased to the old road, and she had only bought to the new one. Since the ten-foot strip was no-man's-land, I immediately filed on it and thus settled that dispute.

Do It Now

Now I began to wonder why I had put myself in such a situation that people were threatening to shoot me, and if that didn't work, to burn us out. If I were a criminal or had done something wrong, it would have been easier to understand, but all I wanted to do was to start a boys' ranch.

It wasn't going to be easy, that I was certain. But optimist that I am, I believed the problems would soon be resolved. Had I known at that time of all the heartaches and trials of the future, I would have been emotionally unable to continue toward the dream. I knew the day of miracles was not past, but I had no idea that the Lord would have to intervene so many times, in so many ways.

After graduation from college I spent a year in juvenile probation work and had been in elementary education ever since. Although I enjoyed teaching immensely, it also had its drawbacks—the long hours of preparation and relatively low pay. But its assets were also abundant. I especially enjoyed the flexible summer program that allowed me to take additional schooling or follow other interests. Most summers I spent a week or two at one of the nearby youth camps.

Pinecrest Summer Camp held a special place in my life, as my wife, Marlene, and I had met there eight years previously. Usually I served as a counselor, but this particular time they needed help with maintenance, so I had a private tent. Crafts and canoeing filled the days for the campers, and building and repairing kept me busy. One by one they slipped by, and I was eager to get back home to my wife, son, and two foster daughters.

Thursday night I prepared for bed with some anticipation, as I had made arrangements with the camp director to return home for the weekend to hear Marlene's trio sing a song I had written. As I knelt beside my bed I heard a voice. It probably wouldn't have been audible to anyone else had they been there, but it was the closest thing to a supernatural voice that I have ever experienced. Simply three words, "Do it now." They were distinct and commanding.

Arising from my knees, I thought, "This can't be happening to me. I must be tired." However, I clearly understood the intent of the voice . . . I was to start a school for youth that otherwise might never learn to know Jesus Christ. Years before, Marlene and I had discussed it as a possibility and then discarded the idea as impractical.

Not being delirious or even sleepy, I returned to my knees. I did not for a moment entertain a "no" answer, only that others must be better able and better prepared to do the work. Money was another problem, and like a lot of other young couples, we "owed all we earned."

That night I spent communing with Someone that was a lot more interested in young people than I was, until at 4:30 in the morning and still on my knees, I promised the Lord that if He would lead the way, I would, indeed, "Do it now." That's all He asked, and immediately a deep peace, such as I had never known, came over me. I slipped into bed and instantly fell asleep.

The morning call sounded two hours later, and much to my surprise, I wasn't even tired or sleepy. Quite to the contrary, the elation was still present, and I could hardly wait to see how the Lord would fulfill His end of our partnership.

When noon arrived I packed my clothes and drove down the winding mountain road toward home. Anticipation bubbled from every pore, and as I often do when I travel, I sang at the top of my voice. Accompanied by the engine's purr, Bing Crosby couldn't have sounded better.

Speeding around the curves beside the American River, as I had done dozens of times before, I was oblivious to my surroundings. I happened to glance across the river on one particular stretch of the road, and there on the beautiful Forbes Ranch stood a "For Sale" sign. It may have been there before, but I had never seen it.

The Forbes Ranch was a landmark from my earliest recollections. It had two large stone lodges, a caretaker's cottage, and shops. The gardens, with their red, orange, and yellow flowers, sloped to the river between the highway and the lodges and were showing some signs of neglect. There stretched the picturesque bridge crossing the river. But it all seemed too ideal to be within my price range. I couldn't even consider speaking to anyone about it. And yet, somehow, I felt impressed that the place would play a part in the development of a boys' ranch. By this time I had driven a mile or more past the ranch, but on impulse I turned around and went back to get the address and phone number of the realtor. Fortunately, it proved to be right on my way home, and I soon stood across the desk from the realtor.

"I noticed your sign at the Forbes Ranch," I began. "What is the asking price?"

Being fairly familiar with the high prices of other properties along the river, I was totally unprepared for his answer. "A church group has decided to let it go for forty-five thousand dollars," he said.

Swallowing, I tried to remain calm. I had expected the price to be more than twice that amount. With as much poise and assumed confidence as I could muster, I replied, "All right, I'll take it. Draw up the papers, and I'll be back Monday to sign them." With that announcement, I left the office. Now that that was settled, all I had to do was go out and find forty-five thousand dollars. I didn't even have one hundred dollars, but I was confident that God would in some way provide the funds, and I fairly flew on toward home.

The closer I got to home, the more concerned I became about a very real problem that loomed ahead. It was fine for me to be committed to a task, but I began to worry about my family. While I knew that my two-year-old son couldn't care less, I wasn't so sure about his mother. I was afraid of what her attitude might be. At times she seemed quite in favor of another dozen boys in the home, and at other times she strongly opposed it.

As I drove the remaining fifty miles I kept praying, "Lord, I won't hold back anything, but You know it's going to take two of us. Somehow, You're going to have to convince Marlene of this project."

Little did I realize that God had answered my prayer even before I had begun to pray.

"Hi, Honey," I greeted her, trying to appear calm above excited shouts and giggles, hugs and kisses, from the three little ones. Then added, "I've got something to tell you," as my enthusiasm started to spill over.

"And I've got something to tell you," she spoke calmly as she continued ironing matching frilly pink dresses for the girls. "You bought a boys' ranch."

"Who . . . ? How . . . !" I stammered. "The realtor must have called."

"No, no one called," she answered softly, with a touch of reverence. "I dreamed last night we started a boys' ranch. The place had two large lodges, and it had beautiful trees, gardens, an orchard . . ."

I could hardly have described the Forbes Ranch better myself. *God knows my needs before I even ask.*

The next step was to find someone willing to donate one thousand dollars for an idea that wasn't even on paper. I thought first of Caris Simons, an old friend of mine who owned a large business on the outskirts of town. Lodi isn't a big town, but the folks are a hardworking, industrious group who retain that pleasant, small-town friendliness. Caris' business had prospered remarkably well in recent years, and I felt that surely he could spare the money. With a prayer in my heart, I walked confidently into his office.

"Caris," I began, "I need a thousand dollars for a down payment."

"I need ten dollars," he chuckled.

"No, I'm serious. I feel the Lord is definitely calling and leading me to do a work for young boys."

With that introduction, I went into the details, of the need for a home for boys who require a little extra supervision and encouragement and of our plans to provide the stability they must have. He listened intently, and when I finished with my enthusiastic little speech, he sat back, stroked his chin, and slowly began.

"Well, Carl, it sounds like a good plan, but it will never work. Others have tried it and failed, and I just hate to put my money down a rathole. Now if you are somehow able to make it work, come and see me, and then I'll help you."

I wasn't angry, but my reply was rather definite. "It isn't a question of *if*, Caris; it's only a question of *when*, and I'll be back!" And with that positive note, I left.

I wasn't discouraged. I would go to every

Do It Now

home in Lodi if necessary. The Lord would provide the money, but I didn't have many hours left before Monday morning. Various names came to mind, wealthy friends and then some less wealthy, generous ones.

Go see L. P. West. Why, of course. They had been friends of my family for years.

Mr. West greeted me cordially at the door. "Come in, Carl. Have a seat." After a brief visit with him and his wife, I explained my mission. They listened intently without commenting. My need stated, I paused. "Could you come back Sunday?" He straightened in his chair and scratched a note on his calendar. "It sounds like a good plan, but we would like to think it over and pray about it before making any decision."

I assured them that I would return on Sunday, and after a short prayer together I left.

At home we offered more prayers for guidance and blessing. On Sunday morning I was eager to return to the Wests' home and get their decision. Feeling certain I knew what their answer would be, I hadn't contacted anyone else about our dream project.

Mr. West met me at the door and invited me in. "Carl," he began as he walked over to his desk and opened the drawer, "here's a check for one thousand dollars. I want to help you as someone once helped me. His help enables us to fulfill our dream here, so I'm just passing the help along."

Even though I was sure that the Lord would

work through him, it was exciting to see it happen, and I was deeply grateful.

Our plan was progressing faster than I had at first believed it would. "If it's going to be this easy, why didn't I do it long ago?" I thought to myself. How little I knew what sacrifices and trials would be required in order to "do it now."

Chapter 2

Little Dividends

Everywhere I went people asked the same questions: "What does it look like? What facilities are available?"

Since most people hesitate to give for an "intangible" idea, pictures were a real necessity. We spent the last of our funds on film and a trip to the ranch to get the required photographs. Upon our return I took the exposed film to a local camera store for developing. The clerk assured me that the prints would be ready the following Wednesday.

Wednesday arrived, and I went to pick up the pictures. Although I still didn't have any money, I had planned to ask for credit. "No," the clerk said, "I just don't understand it. They should have been here today, but they're not. Can you come back tomorrow? I'm sure we'll have them by then."

Disappointed, I left and returned Thursday—and Friday. The pictures still weren't in, but I still didn't have any money either.

In Saturday's mail we received a letter bearing an unfamiliar postmark. Opening it I found a short note and check from a woman I had changed a tire for on the freeway. Although I have always tried to help any motorist in need, and many have offered to pay me, I have never accepted, and instead use the opportunity to witness and encourage them. Perplexed at the unexpected donation, I asked Marlene how the woman could have known our address.

"Well," she replied, "while you were changing her tire, the woman asked where we were going. I just naturally told her all about the boys' ranch, and she asked for our address."

It was Philippians 4:19 all over again. Monday when the camera shop opened, I went to get the pictures. They were in, and the unexpected money was sufficient to pay for them.

Now that we had pictures, a brochure was obviously the next step. We had to have something to leave with the people I met that would explain our dream. Something to show the facilities and explain our goals and, hopefully, serve as a reminder that the boys' ranch needed their help and prayers. Funds didn't allow for a professional artist, so I spent many hours designing, arranging, and rearranging pictures while praying that the Lord would guide my mind and hands.

As expensive as the brochure was going to be, I knew that God would somehow supply our needs as He had promised to do. So, with a dollar in our bank account, I gave the proposed

Little Dividends

brochure to the printer and promised to pay him when it was ready. I really had no idea where we would get the necessary funds.

School was just starting, and I had agreed to teach in Lodi for one last year to enable our corporation to get underway. As I prepared my room for the new term, organizing the library and rearranging the desks, the principal approached me. "Carl," he said, "we have a little problem. You know I don't like for teachers to drive bus in addition to their classroom duties, but our No. 2 driver will be a week late, and I was wondering if you would fill in for her until she gets back."

Already I had more than I really needed to do, with school opening and my plans and work toward the ranch. Although it meant leaving home earlier and getting home later, it also meant extra money to apply toward the printing bill, so I readily agreed.

More funds were not long in coming. The funeral home called and asked me to sing at a service for someone I didn't even know. Although I had sung at many funerals, it was always for friends or relatives, and I wouldn't think of accepting pay in such situations. However, since I was not acquainted with this person or his family, I accepted the envelope and eagerly added it to the printing fund.

Then the church secretary called and asked if I would consider singing for a wedding reception. The couple was from Germany and, although unknown to me, apparently had relatives in town. Gratefully I accepted monetary thanks. It, too, entered the expense funds. More unexpected moneys followed. The bus driving that was to last one week continued for nearly six weeks and then added to that was another funeral and some other extras.

One day as we were going through the receipts, I added up all the extra expenditures, such as the brochure, film processing, and receipt and record books, and then all the "extra" money that had come in unexpectedly. I found that I was sixteen cents in the black. And I am just naive enough to believe that even that may have been an error on my part, such as not including tax or something. God always does things precisely.

Deadlines seemed to pile up quickly. I remained too busy at school to devote as much time to the ranch project as I would have liked. But I didn't feel that the school program should be allowed to suffer because of my extracurricular activities. My room topped the other rooms by two hundred dollars at the Pet and Hobby Show, our Second Annual Science Fair drew quite a crowd, and one of our projects won recognition in the local newspaper. My English classes published the first school paper, and the first hardcover school annual ever put out by our school was a real success in spite of some of the older teachers who said, "It will never work." Several people were still arguing that boys' ranching was a lost cause, but the Lord was still

Little Dividends

leading, and I had faith that if it was to be a success to His glory, it would be.

More deadlines passed. I was tired—physically and mentally. Then on Friday the weekly *Adventist Review* came. It contained an article about a boys' ranch that did make it. It gave me the boost I really needed, and I returned to work with more vigor and renewed determination.

Having visited and read about numerous youth ranches and homes across the country, I was well aware of the need for an organization. In an effort to profit from their mistakes, I also talked with personnel from many ranches and schools that had closed for one reason or another. A recurring problem with the "failures" was the lack of organization, and I determined to build the foundation correctly. I wanted a progressive program and, not knowing what the future held, one that would continue whether or not I was involved.

I called a successful businessman friend. "Jerry," I asked, "do you know of any good attorneys that you could recommend? We're trying to organize this boys' ranch corporation, and we need some good legal advice."

"Yes, we do have a new attorney who just moved to Lodi," he replied. "And from what I understand, he's very good. His name is Tom."

Greatly interested, I inquired, "Do you know if he married a local girl?"

"Yes," he said, "I think he did." I was elated.

Although Tom and I were classmates at Loma Linda University and I had grown up with his wife, I had no idea that he was an attorney or that they had moved back to Lodi.

The board suggested a few names for the corporation and then strongly insisted it bear my nickname, Mr. A, which had originated some years earlier when a three-year-old foster boy couldn't say Anderson. We had shortened it for him, and he translated it to "Misser A." Mr. A stuck with me in the classroom. Although I had no objections to the name, as such, I felt the name for the ranch should reflect a work, not a person. However, they outvoted me, and the official name became Mr. A's Boys' Ranch.

Within weeks Tom had the organization underway. On November 28, 1966, Mr. A's Boys' Ranch, Inc. was officially incorporated as a corporation of the State of California. The corporate seal arrived a few weeks later, and everyone had to try the new gadget by "sealing" newspapers and magazines.

Our next big hurtles were the State Franchise Tax Board and the Internal Revenue Service for nonprofit status. A lot of prayer went with our filling out the necessary forms. Then we waited—and prayed.

An architect went with me to the property and drew up the first plans for the conversion of the buildings. His plans were most exciting. I pictured landscaping the property, flowers along the riverbank—it would be a beautiful landmark.

Little Dividends

The local Kiwanis Club called to ask about the project, which resulted in the first of hundreds of presentations before service clubs, churches, and other organizations. It was a breakfast meeting, and they would allow me twenty minutes. The president made it very clear to me: "These men have to leave for work promptly at 8:35."

I spoke for the allotted twenty minutes, then asked for questions. Many pledged financial and material support. Others gave names of people with means who would be interested. They were still asking questions at 9:30.

It was such a wonderful start that I wondered if anything could possibly go wrong. How thankful I am that a merciful God had hidden the future from view.

Chapter 3

Wandering in the Wilderness

March 20 dawned bright and clear after what seemed like weeks of rain and overcast. We had the rest of the down payment ready to make on the Forbes Ranch the following day. That evening one of my board members called. "Carl," he said, "I was just told about some property near Jackson that may be available, and I'd like you to check it out before we actually get into the Forbes Ranch."

I told him I would do it the next morning and let him know. Although I was certain that we were not interested, I felt it my duty to honor his request. The next morning I drove out to find the "ranch."

The "This Is Your Life" television program had bought the large acreage for an ex-con who had "gone straight" and was interested in helping boys. I easily found the place, or what was left of it—one small run-down house, a block building twenty feet by sixteen feet, with walls four feet high. That was all.

The owner said that the "gone-straight ex-

Wandering in the Wilderness 25

con" had hired as his manager the famous "great impostor." He had a few boys for a while trying to build this block building, but they lived in tents and spent their recreation periods stealing anything and everything from the neighbors. "No, this property isn't for sale," he sighed, "but it sounds like the place down the road is something you might be interested in."

Happy Valley Ranch proved to be a beautiful place. White board fences lined the road, and a small creek bubbled through the pasture and on to the river. Horses grazed on the lush green fields that surrounded a large stable and corrals. The house was a castlelike structure with yellow shutters and a red tile roof. The doors were solid oak, three inches thick, and made with wooden pegs. An enormous oak tree shaded the backyard. Large boulders dotted with potholes gave evidence of Indians having camped nearby. The setting was beautiful and would be a lovely place for a boys' ranch.

Looking at the picturesque valley ranch, I did not realize that this "wonderful opportunity" was the beginning of a "wandering in the wilderness" experience instead of the answer to our dreams.

The board felt impressed that Happy Valley suited our needs better than the Forbes Ranch on the American River. For one thing, it was more remote and had more acreage, so negotiations proceeded. Our attorney drew up the three-page, double-spaced "agreement of sale" that both parties had consented to, and I took it to the realtor.

The realtor took it to the owners for approval. They, in turn, sent back a twelve-page, single-spaced lease agreement instead of a purchase as we had agreed to, outlining forty-six whereas's: "lease subject to, condition of premises, could be used only for . . . and not for destruction of premises, condemnation of premises, alterations" and so on. It was very complicated and confusing, but in laymen's language one could translate it as "We want to lease only, and then only if you want to do it our way." The restrictions and strings closed the door on Happy Valley Ranch.

So, we had let the Forbes Ranch go in favor of Happy Valley. Now we had lost Happy Valley due to strings. Once again I visited every realtor along the Sierra foothills looking for the right place. People gave suggestions: "Someone told me about . . ." or, "I read about a ranch. . . ." I checked every lead and wasted a lot of my time, gas, and nerves, but I felt that it was necessary and important to do my part by checking out every possibility.

We placed an ad in a paper with a wide circulation, requesting property for a boys' ranch. The response was almost zero. A postcard stated, "St. Helena Hospital was willed some property. See them."

Another told us, "We have five acres for which we are asking five thousand dollars but will sell to you for three thousand."

Wandering in the Wilderness 27

The third and final response to our ad read, "I am looking for a home for my disturbed nephew."

And so the search continued.

One day a realtor with more zeal than honesty showed me a beautiful piece of property with a twenty-acre lake, an abundance of trees, and a few buildings. The board made a trip to look at the lake property and decided it was indeed the place, so I proceeded to deposit a thousand dollars with the realtor, "subject to approval by the county planning commission to use said property for a boys' ranch."

Then one afternoon I went with the realtor to the planning commission office to check out any zoning restrictions. The clerk at the office was congenial and seemed interested in our plans for a boys' ranch. He asked many questions, which I eagerly answered.

"You realize, of course," he began, "the water rights don't . . ."

"You keep out of this," the realtor shouted and motioned to me that we were ready to leave. "I'm selling this property, and when I need your help I'll ask for it."

I walked with the realtor to where our cars were parked, and he got in his and drove away. As soon as he was gone, I went back to the planning commission office. "Now, what was it you started to say about water rights?" I asked.

"Well"—he straightened the papers on his desk—"I just wanted to make sure you realized that Baron's Lake is controlled by the irrigation district, and there is a distinct possibility of using it for domestic purposes in the future. Of course, it may be several years from now, but they do control it."

"What would that mean to our plans for the property?" I asked.

"At such time as they should elect to use it for domestic water supply, they would put a fence around it, and you couldn't even stick your big toe in it. Somehow I felt you weren't aware of this."

"You're right," I assured him, "I wasn't. That's why I wanted to come in today, but the realtor insisted he come with me to make sure I got all the details. This property wouldn't serve our purposes at all with that possibility in mind."

Thanking him for his time and honesty, I met with the board again. Some said yes, we should go ahead and buy Baron's Lake, and others said absolutely not. After much prayer we decided to keep looking. When I notified the realtor that we were aware of the irrigation district restriction, he returned our deposit.

A short time later a realtor drove me to the Murphy Ranch in the heart of Welcome Valley. The one-hundred-acre ranch had a small dam, level acreage for building and agriculture, and a beautiful view across a small valley to pine-covered mountains. A year-round stream ran through the ranch. It seemed to fill all our needs for a boys' ranch.

Totally convinced, I put down two hundred dollars of my own money as a retainer deposit and hurried excitedly to tell the board members. Some were not too thrilled, while others were only passively excited. Most were a little tired of hearing about this place and that. I had to remind them it was at their insistence that we had let the first place go. The board finally voted to at least take a look at the new property. When they saw it, they "knew" our search was over.

But . . . if we had only known.

Chapter 4

Deadline Decisions

We had to consider a lot of things in starting a boys' ranch. For example, we debated the pros and cons of dormitories versus home-style housing, eating cafeteria or family style, and the grade span and admissions policies. Since I had never worked at a youth ranch, I took the opportunity to visit homes for delinquents and homes for retarded individuals, homes operated by churches, and state and private corporations.

The manager-owner of a home for retarded children admonished, "Carl, you're crazy for not going into the home-for-retarded business. There's real money in it. Why, you won't get nothin' for normal kids, and they are more work."

"I realize that this may be very true," I told him, "but our concern is to help boys who have problems so they can go on to be useful citizens of this life and, more important, prepared for eternity."

"But do you know how much money I made last year?" he wanted to know. "Clear?" Of course I had no idea, and when he stated an astronomical figure, it boggled my brain.

"Man, I'll be retired when you're still out there scratching."

And . . . at the date of this writing, he is, and I am . . . still!

Another home, billed as a "Christian" home, had only one boy from a Christian background. The rest were hardcore state delinquents, wards of the court, that couldn't care less about God or anybody else. "Why is it," I questioned, "that your ranch is supported by your church, and yet you don't have any Christian students?"

"We don't accept them," came his curt reply.

"May I ask why?"

"Sure," he said. "It's hard to get money for private students. With the state wards I know there will be a check every month."

"Do the students want to be here, and are their parents cooperative and grateful for what you're trying to do for their sons?"

"Oh, my, no," he grumbled. "These smart-mouth kids would leave here in a minute. Some do run away, but when they get caught, the law hits them harder the next time. As for their parents, no, they don't want them here." He reflected with apparent disgust, "It's some place the authorities sent their kid, and as far as they're concerned, their kid got a bum deal."

It didn't seem very likely that such an institution's influence would lead the boys or their parents to know Jesus Christ.

I talked with more people: pastors, teachers, and parents.

"Carl," one retired pastor advised, "the problem is with working mothers. If you take care of their children, it will just encourage more mothers to work and cause more problems. No, I'm against it."

"But," I countered, "what about the young boys who need help and motivation to get things together?"

"It will never work," he reasoned. "It's a waste of money and time to try."

Talking with a teacher, I assumed he could understand the need for such a home. "Sure, there's a need," he replied, "but we can't save the whole world."

Of course, not everyone was negative to the plan, and many wonderful people helped in many different ways.

With progress finally beginning to move more rapidly, and with high spirits, I visited more of my friends to obtain the rest of the down payment we needed. Somehow we just couldn't quite reach our goal. A call to our treasurer confirmed that we were five hundred dollars short, and the down payment was due the next day.

That evening as I sat at home with our small son, Chip, I kept praying and wondering how the Lord would provide the five hundred dollars. Marlene had offered to stay home, but since there was nothing that she could do except continue praying, I had urged her to attend the bridal

Deadline Decisions 33

shower to which she had been invited.

Suddenly the jingling of the phone interrupted my thoughts. Had anyone else answered, they would have considered it a rather strange call, for the entire conversation on the other end consisted of just one word, *Now*. Thrilled to be in on an answer to prayer, I quickly called Marlene at the shower. "Honey," I told her, "come home right away; our prayers have been answered."

Eight months previously I had gone to visit the widow of a wealthy industrialist who lived across town. Her nurse had met me and sighed, "Carl, she isn't feeling well today. She has her good days and her bad. If it's a bad day, she wants to see no one; if it's a good one, she's her charming self. She hasn't had too many good days recently, though. You'll just have to keep trying." And I did, without success.

Then one evening the nurse called me from her home. "I've got a great idea. Next time she has a good day, I'll get her in her chair and looking nice and wheel her into the living room. Then I'll go to her bedroom, turn on the air conditioner, make lots of noise, and dial your number. I'll say 'Now,' and you had better hurry."

Marlene met me in the driveway as I left the house and hurried to the widow's house. Knocking on her door, I said a prayer for the five hundred dollars and waited.

She was just as charming and gracious as I had heard she was when she felt well, and her interest in our program was enthusiastic. Beaming, she asked about the boys we would have. Then her face saddened. "Carl, I'd love to help, but since I've been sick, my son takes care of all my finances. He only gives me a little spending money." Then she continued, "I do have a small amount, though. Would five hundred dollars help?"

I fairly jumped out of my seat. To us it was another evidence of the Lord's blessing and leading toward our ultimate goal.

Marlene waited for me at the door, with Chip standing beside her. "We were praying. How much did she give?"

"How much did we need?" I asked, handing her the check.

"Did you tell her how much you needed?" my wife whispered as she held the check.

"No," I smiled, "didn't have to. The Holy Spirit did. Isn't that fantastic!"

Early the following morning I called our treasurer and told her the latest "miracle" and added, "Betty, I'll be by in a little while to get a check for the balance of the down payment. Since I already have the five hundred dollars to make up the difference, I'll take it by the bank on my way."

She hesitated, then said slowly, "There isn't that much money in the bank."

"Why not?" I inquired, sure that she must have made a mistake. "Didn't you mail several checks to the bank last week?"

Her voice grew sad and concerned. "Didn't

Deadline Decisions

you hear about the fire? The mail truck burned. Since my personal account is at the same bank, I mailed the ranch checks with my checks. I called the bank, but they said that none of my checks had gotten through. All I got back was a few charred pieces. All first-class mail was destroyed."

Thanking her, I slumped into a chair. I couldn't believe it. I'd never heard of a mail truck burning.

"I'm sure we can ask the people to issue another check," Marlene consoled. "But that will take so much time. 'Old Scratch' is really working overtime, isn't he?"

He certainly was. With a deadline that day, I couldn't possibly get all those checks replaced and drive to the realtor's office too.

I'll call the bank as soon as it opens," I told her, "but if all first-class mail burned, there really isn't much chance, is there? We'll just have to pray about it."

We did, and at one minute after the opening hour I phoned long-distance to the bank and waited breathlessly while the teller checked our account.

When she read the balance I knew that another miracle had taken place. Somehow our checks had survived the fire, and we met the deposit deadline with the title company.

Our troubles were not over, however. The title company didn't like the way the board minutes were written. They wanted it in the form of a resolution. I dashed the sixty miles back to Lodi to get the necessary signatures, drew up a resolution, and then took it to our attorney, who said it was now written properly. Time was running out. We had to have the resolution back to the title company in Placerville before 5.00 PM to keep the contract from being void.

Rather than call a board meeting, I ran all over San Joaquin and El Dorado counties, securing the nine board members' signatures on the resolution, literally flew the sixty miles back to Placerville, and dashed through the door of the title company at 5:00 PM as an officer approached it with his keys in hand to lock the door. Much to my delight, they accepted it, and the property was ours.

Chapter 5

"Blackerry Jam"

With that settled and the ranch purchased, I felt certain that the pace would begin to slacken—but I couldn't have been more wrong. If it wasn't one deadline, it was another, and if it wasn't the ranch, it was the school. Little by little the worries increased until I had a nice case of stomach ulcers.

The doctor put me on a restricted diet and gave me medicines that tasted like I was in the classroom, eating chalk. I couldn't sleep at night because nothing seemed to put out the fire. The days weren't so great either.

One day during a lull I stopped to analyze my situation. I was sure that God was not honored by my abusing my body, regardless of the cause. Furthermore, I reasoned, if He was behind the project, as long as I was doing my part, we couldn't fail. On the other hand, if I was possibly mistaken and He was not leading, I wanted it to fail.

Then a thought came to my mind, something I either heard or dreamed up, but the message was abundantly clear: "Where faith begins, worry ends."

It seemed so simple, I wondered why I hadn't thought of it before. I repeated it over and over in my mind until I had it firmly implanted. Almost immediately I began to feel better, and whenever the temptation to worry tried to crowd into my mind, I reminded myself of the phrase again.

I stopped taking the medicine, and although the deadlines and problems kept piling up, my ulcers became a problem of the past. Faith began!

Now that we owned the property and were finally getting underway with the boys' ranch project, I felt we needed a new brochure describing the new ranch. Snapping pictures of the stream, the dam, and the meadows, I spread out bits of this and that on the living-room floor until I ended up with a brochure that I took to the press. I helped the printer, although I'm not sure how much help I really was, but I did enjoy the change of pace.

"What's Marlene doing today?" the printer shouted above the din of press and machine noises.

"Oh," I yelled back, "she's cranking out a newsletter on our old mimeograph to accompany these brochures."

"Why don't you let me print it?" he suggested. "It wouldn't cost much. I know what a mimeograph is like, especially an old one."

Marlene eagerly typed a copy for the printer, he set up a masthead, and thus began the

"Blackerry Jam"

forerunner of *The Anvil*. We still continue to edit and publish it. The first mailing was 1,029 copies, but our address list soon grew to over 6,000. The magazine continues to grow in scope and quality. One printing idea seemed to lead to another.

One evening as we stopped by the property to pick some of the delicious blackberries that grew along the stream, I got a bright idea. "Why don't we make some jam to give to those who have donated money?" I suggested to Marlene. "I could even print some labels at the printshop."

The idea sparked her enthusiasm. "How about an old-fashioned label?" she laughed excitedly. Our very own "Knotts' Berry Farm" jam.

She put up the jam in pretty half-pint jelly jars, while I printed the labels. "Wild Blackberry Jam From Mr. A's Boys' Ranch." Then we delivered the jam to the folk who had donated to the ranch, and each expressed his appreciation.

"That spinning wheel in the corner adds a rustic touch." Marlene sat admiring the last couple of jars. She picked up one jar and eyed it curiously. "Do you see anything strange about the label?" she asked, a sly grin tugging at the corners of her mouth.

I looked at it. "The spinning wheel does add a special touch," I acknowledged. "Don't you like the colors together?"

"How about the spelling blackerry? It's missing a *b*," she said, holding the jar closer so I could see.

"Oh, no," I moaned as I examined the label. "This time we can't blame the printer. I set the type myself. Oh, well, no one's perfect. Besides, I enjoyed working in the printshop. It was a nice change. Maybe I should have been a printer."

"Maybe not," my wife laughed. "I don't know if there would be many calls for 'blackerry' jam labels or not."

Thankfully, no one noticed the misspelling, or else they were too kind to mention it. Not even the printer commented about it. A little later I discovered why. Perhaps we should have joined together in a partnership.

We thought membership cards would be a good idea for initial and continued financial support, so we designed a card and took it to the printer. A covered wagon on the background carried out our Western theme. The printer delivered five thousand cards with the word *privilege* misspelled "privelege." Apologizing profusely, he volunteered to make more cards and spell the word correctly. He did—sort of. The second printing, under the line for the treasurer's signature had it spelled "treasure." So we had ten thousand cards and a choice of which misspelled card to send to which member. I didn't really mind, however, and was grateful for his kind help.

Chapter 6

"Where Your Treasure Is . . ."

In spite of pleas from the school board to stay on another year and an offer to become principal of the school, I terminated my teaching career in Lodi at the end of the school year. Of course, my salary also stopped.

We rented a storage garage in a rather shabby neighborhood across town and prepared to move out of our lovely home, which was, and still is, one of the nicest houses in town. As we put our belongings into the garage, we prayed that God would guard our unprotected things. He never let us down.

Our board president expressed concern about where we would live and insisted we stay in a small house he had for sale—rent free. That proved to be a wonderful blessing—no rent, only food and utilities. Except that the money from my last check didn't last long after renting the garage and paying our utility bills at the big house.

Finally we decided to have a garage sale and dispose of some things we didn't really need. We rummaged through the garage and loaded our station wagon with baby furniture and clothes, lots of odds and ends, and miscellaneous furniture that made our garage sale a success and enabled us to pay the utilities and buy food for another month.

During the weeks we camped in the rent-free house I drove to Welcome Valley almost every day. At last we decided we could do more and do it faster if we were closer to the ranch. Driving nearly two hundred miles each day was eating up our meager grocery money much faster than we were.

Financially, we were broke, but we had good hopes for the future. We had sold a small piece of property on the Bear River and, thinking of the future of boys' helping with the ranching, put the money in a small, used mobile home that we had delivered to the ranch property. However, due to the fact that we didn't as yet have the rezoning permit, we didn't dare spend even one night in the trailer for fear of jeopardizing our plans for a boys' ranch in Welcome Valley.

"Maybe we should trade the station wagon in on a pickup and camper," I suggested slyly to Marlene. I didn't tell her I had already been looking for and found a used Chevy pickup with a small camper.

My wife tossed the idea around in her head. "Maybe you'd save enough in gas running back and forth and on utilities here at the house to make the payments."

I agreed and took her to see the camper I had in mind. It was small—four by eight feet—but adequate for the three of us. "After all," I told her, "it is only going to be temporary." How little I knew.

After taking out a personal loan for the pickup, I borrowed an extra four hundred dollars to make the first payment on the ranch property. The payment was already a few days delinquent because the corporation was again out of money. Then we packed our few essentials into the camper and cleaned Mr. Frank's house and yard. "What about the utilities?" Marlene asked. "We don't have any money to pay them."

Sure enough. My salary check was long gone, as was the money from our recent garage sale. "Is there anything else we could sell?" I asked. "Folk here really go for garage sales."

"I can't think of anything else I really want to sell," Marlene replied thoughtfully. "But we could look in the garage again. There's probably something we don't need."

There was. Quite a bit, in fact, and we had special prayer about our garage sale. The Lord answered our prayers, and we got enough money to pay the utilities plus some extra money for gas and food until our next sale.

My grandmother was a praying woman and always a strong Christian influence as I was growing up. Now Chip enjoyed her love and sweet Christian spirit. "Why don't you kids stay here till you get things settled?" she insisted.

"You don't have a shower or toilet in your camper. I know it's hard."

So Grandma opened her home and her heart to us. But we were still too far from the action, so after a couple of weeks we drove toward the ranch in search of a homesite for our camper. We found it, out in the woods twenty miles from the ranch, on the bank of a small creek shaded by enormous ponderosa- and sugar-pine trees.

Marlene and I set up camp, and I continued to raise what few funds I could while we waited for our rezoning permit from the planning commission. In spite of the beautiful setting, the inconveniences were painfully present. I didn't mind the lack of electric lights so much, but the cold fall nights had turned our stream-bathtub into an icebox, and the lack of any toilet facilities left something to be desired also. Without having any clear alternative, due to the sale of the small house we had used rent free, however, we adjusted as well as we could and at times even enjoyed the brisk water.

On our trips back to Lodi to raise money or to consult our attorney, we enjoyed brief visits with Grandma. Her good cooking and much-needed encouragement and the little boxes of food she sent back with us, especially her Danish cookies, kept us going. She kept saying in her Danish accent, "If I vus younger, I'd be right in dare vit you. Wictory comes from trying." So with her box of goodies and her best wishes and prayers and often a "love gift" for gas, we returned to the

"Where Your Treasure Is . . ."

foothills strengthened to fight new battles.

The boys' ranch wasn't going anyplace, and money was scarce. Besides our gas and food expenses, we paid thirty dollars a month on the storage garage. To get money we decided to have an antique sale on Grandma's porch. Our antiques included pitcher and bowl sets, our collection of butter molds, apple peelers, pitcher pumps, and a wide variety of other antiques we had collected over the years. The Lord blessed the sale, and her front porch became a favorite porch-sale spot.

Soon another payment came due. By now I had even run out of money for gas. "Honey," I told Marlene one day, "we're going to have to sell some more of our antiques. We have to have some money, and it just isn't coming in."

I can honestly say I wasn't too excited about selling collections that had taken years to gather, along with some items that had passed down from our ancestors.

"We have some glassware and the purple candlesticks," she sighed thoughtfully. "Actually, there's probably quite a bit of stuff we could sell—especially when you think of it in terms of survival and success."

I knew we were both trying to convince ourselves. Once again we prayed that the Lord would bless our sale.

"How much do you want for your pitcher and bowl set?" I asked. I couldn't put a price on her treasure.

"Frankly, I really don't want to sell it." She turned her head. "You sell it for what you think it's worth, but don't tell me what you got for it—ever!" It sold, and I promptly "forgot" the price, for with those heirlooms, the "price" was more than money.

At our home on the creek, Marlene and Chip were alone from early until late almost every day while I visited neighbors around the ranch and worked with the county. It all seemed so endless and time consuming.

Chip, however, enjoyed every moment, playing in the water, collecting pinecones, rocks, and all the other things a three-year-old boy accumulates. I moved some rocks in the bottom of the creek and made a hole deep enough for him to wade in. The water was much too cold for him to sit in, but he played contentedly all day, only requiring a drink, food, and answers to his questions now and then.

"I've never seen you look so tired," Marlene commented as I came home one evening after another hard day. "You have no idea how many times I pray for you during the day. I pray you will be kept safe but also that you'll have courage and strength and wisdom. It's hard on me," she sighed. "I can't possibly imagine how hard it is on you."

God had, indeed, given me courage and strength, I told her, and I recalled how He had also sent His angels to protect me, not only from the irate neighbor's threats to shoot me but on

"Where Your Treasure Is . . ."

the highway as well.

I had been driving a little faster than reasonable on the freeway, slick from a recent rain. As I approached the crest of a hill and a curve, the bald tires became hydrofoils, and I headed for the cliff to the right of the road. Desperately I turned the wheel but to no avail. All I had time to say was, "Jesus, Jesus," and the car immediately settled on the edge of the right-hand lane. No doubt exists in my mind that the hand of God brought the car back to the freeway with but inches to spare.

Later in the fall we went to a flea market and sold a pickup load of antiques: a round oak stove, a spinning wheel, and boxes and boxes of things we really didn't "need." People often asked, "How do you manage financially?" When I told them, they would shake their heads and say, "I don't know how you can sell all your possessions."

"No," I always assured them. "We haven't sold any possessions—just a few accumulations."

It wasn't easy, but the Lord blessed our sales. We will always remember one trip to the flea market. The garage rent was due, plus a loan payment, and, as usual, we needed money for gas and food. We didn't have or expect any extras. Laying our problem before the Lord, we reminded Him of the amount of money we needed to meet our expenses. Fully believing that we were doing His will, we depended completely on Him for our existence, meager though it was.

People passed our booth, interested in everything we had but buying little. By 1:00 in the afternoon, when most of the items should have been gone, we had sold only twenty-seven dollars' worth. Marlene got tired, physically and emotionally, standing there talking to the bargain hunters, quoting and requoting prices. Discouraged, she said, "I think I'll take a quick nap. Would you care?"

I didn't care. There wasn't much going on, so I really didn't need her help anyway.

When she came out of the camper after a nap, I could hardly wait to show her our tables. "Hey, Honey, almost as soon as you left, people started coming by and buying. They bought all of the big stuff, and this is all that's left. Maybe you better take another nap."

"I noticed," she grinned. "Before I lay down, I prayed that the Lord would bless our sale. I dozed and prayed again, then slept, and when I woke up, I prayed again." She peeked into the cashbox. "I came out cautiously. First I looked out the window to see if anything was gone. Practically everything is gone. He really did answer."

It was a relief for me that she was back to help. I couldn't keep up with the constant inquiries and the rapid sales of the last few items.

Chapter 7

In Spite of Us

Growing up in a home where prayer is a daily way of life, I found it is a thrill as well as a challenge. As our faith grows and develops and our walk with God becomes closer, our attitudes and requests change from one of "gimme, gimme," and almost presumption, to one of "thank You, Lord" and praise.

At sixteen I went through a stage in my life in which nothing seemed to move fast enough. I wanted to make things happen. In a way it was probably a kind of salvation by works, although I didn't realize it at the time. God knew my heart, however, and often answered even those problems I had gotten myself into by my own stupidity.

I wasn't what you would call really bad, but I just enjoyed a good practical joke. Even today I remember the nickel I affixed to a nail and pounded into the wooden steps, or the disappearing purse in the street, the explosive that would detonate upon impact when dropped from a second-story window, the bag of mud that plummeted from nowhere upon the head, the dummy-in-the-bed routine, or a lot of other nondestructive (except to one's pride and composure) jokes.

I had just gotten my driver's license. "Wheels," I thought, were just about the greatest thing ever invented. Not having an excess of funds, we didn't drive just for the fun of it, but we coveted the opportunity when there was some place to go.

My grandparents lived in a nearby town, and we often drove to visit them until one day, after a short illness, my grandfather suddenly passed away. Since the funeral was scheduled for 2:00 PM, my parents left early to enable them to be with the rest of the family before the service, while I was to come a little later and bring a carload of my brothers and cousins. It seemed that everyone was a little late. By the time my car was loaded, we had just enough time to make the short trip before the funeral began.

I took a shortcut to save time and completely forgot about the weeks of torrential rain and flooding that inundated our section of California. As I rounded the last big curve in the road, I felt a sinking feeling in the pit of my stomach. In front of me, less than a mile from our destination, water covered the long bridge and for a distance on each side. If I turned and went around the other way, my brothers, cousins, and I would be too late for the service, an unforgivable sin in our family. On the other hand, if I attempted to drive through, and the water was too deep, we would still miss it. That's when I should have prayed instead of trying to work it out myself.

About that time a car drove around the corner on the far side of the water, took one look at the water, and turned around and went back. Suddenly I got an idea. Turning the car around, I backed a few feet into the water's edge and waited. A few minutes later as another car came around the corner on the far side of the flood, I slowly drove out of the water.

The other car, thinking that I had safely crossed the bridge, plunged into the flooded road. At first it felt like a stroke of genius, but then realizing what I had done, I started praying for their safety. I didn't know how deep the water was or even if the bridge was still there. At any moment I half expected to see the car disappear from sight or at least "short" out in the deep water. Thankfully, the car crossed safely, whereupon, I turned my car around and did the same.

Somehow, I survived my childhood, in spite of myself, and even enjoyed it.

A sustaining faith is probably the prime ingredient to a happy and successful life, and my family developed an abundant measure. Prayer had been a way of life, all of my life, and my parents were ardent practitioners. Although qualified to teach anywhere, they chose to spend their lives serving in parochial schools where Jesus Christ was more than a mere historical figure.

After spending a number of years in the classroom, they developed the "classroom fatigue" so common among veteran teachers. At the close of the term, they decided to enter another line of work. Offered an attractive position with a box factory near Valley Springs, California, Dad eagerly entered into his new occupation. The pay was good for the 1930s, and at first, the future seemed bright.

With the passing of the harvest season and the worldwide depression deepening, business didn't merely start to fall off, it just plain stopped. The company that had but a few months before looked so promising was not able to pay its weekly salaries. After Dad had lived three weeks on promises, the factory superintendent approached him and told him the factory was bankrupt.

"Well," Dad replied, "I'm glad you told me. Your timing isn't the greatest, though. School's been on for a month, and it's hard to get a job."

But my parents' faith didn't waver, and they made their plight a matter of urgent prayer to the Lord. Since they had come to the factory to "get a little ahead," they felt somewhat like Jonah in leaving the work that God had called them into, but they knew that He had not deserted them.

A car drove into the factory yard, and a man in a business suit got out and inquired as to the whereabouts of Victor and Mary Anderson. When Dad saw the man, he knew that he, the superintendent of schools, was the answer to

In Spite of Us

their prayers. One small problem remained in that the school district he represented did not have funds to move them. Dad thanked him and told him they would get there somehow.

More prayers for guidance and of gratefulness ascended, and then Dad remembered an old miner working the Calaveras River, several miles back of the factory. My parents drove to the river and explained their predicament to the miner. "Sure," he said, "just get yourself an old frying pan and swish the gravel around like this, and you'll find some gold." They did as he told them and in a few days had gathered enough placer gold to pay for their move to the new school.

Additional years went by with successful teaching in various California schools until another bout with classroom fatigue occurred. Dad decided to go to work for his brother, who ran a pest-control business. The flourishing business began at once to drop off. My father had received a letter from the school board begging them to return for the next term. As the business continued to decline, they made it a matter of considerable prayer and finally told the board that they would come. That same day the pest-control company received one of its largest jobs. It not only paid for the move back to the school in southern California but provided for some of the extras they had been needing. The pest-control company, incidentally, continued to expand until it required a number of additional men to handle the volume of business. And Dad and

Mom were back in the classroom.

The third time my father quit the classroom, he bought a ranch near Sacramento and went to work at McClellan Field. Although he enjoyed the work, he knew he was not where the Lord wanted him to be. One day when he had this feeling, he went into the storeroom and knelt behind some wooden pallets. "Lord," he prayed, "if You want me to go back into teaching, impress someone to give me an invitation. I'm not going to pursue the job, but if someone calls, I'll go." With the future in the Lord's hands, he was at peace the rest of the day.

When Dad returned home that evening, my mother met him at the door with, "Guess whom we had a call from today?" After he had related his prayer to her, they found that the call to teach had come at the same time as he prayed. We all understood God's plan and eagerly made preparations for another move. Within a month we had sold the ranch, moved, and were comfortable in our new home in Lodi.

From that time on Dad didn't step out of the classroom until his retirement, and he still holds one foot in the door as a substitute teacher.

Mom died nearly twenty years later knowing that two of her sons were already teaching and that I was preparing to enter the field. But before she passed to her rest, she wrote me a personal letter that I still treasure. She dealt with family things and some of the experiences that I have shared, then closed with, "I have a very strong impression that you will not be a history teacher, even if that's what you major in. I believe the Lord is leading and preparing you for a place in His youth work."

I guess she must have been right.

Chapter 8

The "Piece" Makers

I had driven down to Lodi to pick up a few things and was visiting at the home of a board member when the phone rang. "It's for you," Frank said. "I think it's the realtor."

After a few words of greeting, our realtor got down to the purpose of his call. "It probably isn't anything serious, but I thought you ought to know. It's been rumored that there may be some opposition at the hearing to rezone the property for boys' ranch use." Bud spoke with a sense of urgency and concern in his voice. "Perhaps you should come up and talk to the neighbors and straighten things out."

"Thanks for calling, Bud," I replied. "I'll be right up."

It was a surprising new development, and we hoped and prayed that our plans and dreams wouldn't be thwarted now. During the past few weeks things had been going surprisingly well.

The property had loomed up in apparent answer to our prayers for the right place to start a boys' ranch in the Sierra foothills. It all added up

The "Piece" Makers

to a fine place for orphans and boys who needed a temporary home away from home. A place where a boy could ride a horse, chase lizards, swim, hike—it was the place as far as we were concerned.

But perhaps things were going too well for our own good and the ultimate success of our goals. At any rate, here was a development that we had not anticipated. If there was any possibility of averting or avoiding setbacks and delays, we were anxious to do whatever necessary. After prayer for traveling protection and wisdom in dealing with the matter, I left, anticipating the worst, yet hoping for the best.

At Welcome Valley, Bud related what he knew about a petition circulating in the area, as well as a busy-body neighbor woman, which might prevent the county planning commission for rezoning the property for our purposes. I decided to do a house-to-house survey and disprove any false stories.

The residents of the first house in the small mother-lode community were most gracious when I told them exactly what we planned to do with the property. "Well, that's interesting," the man of the house commented. "Not at all like it was explained to us by our neighbor. She told us you were going to house two hundred mentally retarded juvenile delinquents in house trailers. Of course we weren't in favor of a thing like that in our neighborhood. It didn't even sound sane. We're sure glad to know the truth. The lady down the road tends to tell things a little dishonestly."

At the conclusion of our conversation, the couple volunteered to sign a petition in favor of our program, expressed their regrets, and wished us good luck as I went on my way. I needed their good-luck wishes perhaps more than they realized and certainly more than I ever dreamed.

The next contact turned out to be not quite so pleasant. Two couples were playing cards, and according to my sense of sight, sound, and smell, the one couple were quite drunk. The man became verbally abusive of our plan, of me personally (whom he had never seen before), the county, the city, the federal government, and the whole world. It took some doing to get him to stop long enough so I could make my exit.

As I walked to my car, the visiting couple hurriedly followed. "Don't worry about them. We're all for you and will support you in any way we can." It was a welcome contrast to the response I had received in the house.

Although I tried to explain to the people at the next house that the rumor wasn't true, they had other varied and nonsensical objections. "You gonna bring in any niggers?" the irate man of the house demanded.

"Well," I responded, fishing around for a diplomatic answer, "we just want to give help to boys who need it."

"Don't want no blacks 'round here. No, sir. We're ag'in it. We signed the petition, and we're

The "Piece" Makers

still ag'in it."

Obviously his mind was made up, and he didn't want to be confused with facts.

A Los Angeles ex-policeman lived down the road in the opposite direction. His manner (or lack of) unfortunately was that of the smart-alecky, out-to-get-the-world cop. He would be our neighbor. "After all, that property is where me and my boys goes deer huntin' ever' year," he bellered. "And if you move in, you probably wouldn't let us go deer huntin' by your house."

Everyone I talked to suggested that "the lady" across the road from us had given them the information they had received, tainted though it was. I refer to her as "lady" by way of clarification and gender, not due to her principles or behavior.

When I talked with her, she dominated the conversation with much vulgar profanity and verbal abuse and little reasoning or logic. She knew and recited every adjective and pronoun in the swear book between puffing on her cigarette and yelling at her children, dogs, cats, and the neighborhood. "You'd steal from me, and besides that, my kids goes swimmin' in the pond all the time and pick the plums, and if you moved in they couldn't use that property no more."

After hearing about other residents of Welcome Valley, we had some sympathy for the worry about vandalism and robbery. And when we learned about her family, we were convinced that their concern was justified, if possibly misplaced. And she was worried about us?

The problem seemed insurmountable, but the Lord gave us strength to face even more unbelievable trials.

The day for the hearing finally arrived. Having visited everyone living within a few miles of the property, even though the county ordinance said that only those within five hundred feet were affected, I felt that I had done all I could. My board members had been notified, and some volunteered to be present for the meeting called for 7:30 that evening.

Arriving at the courthouse, where it would take place, I noticed that the parking lot was nearly full, and I wondered what else was going on. However, when I walked into the hearing room, it was evident where all the people were. They filled nearly every seat in the auditorium.

The presiding county supervisor who, unfortunately, was up for reelection, opened the meeting with a political speech designed to impress us with his fairness and honesty. Then I received two minutes to briefly state our purposes, after which the fireworks began. People shouted, some booed, and a few even hissed. I don't think that Adolf Hitler could have orchestrated the demonstration much more effectively. Even though her facts and figures were grossly incorrect and her motives and morals were wrong, "The Lady" had certainly done a sales job on the community. Perhaps even "community" is an incorrect term, for she had brought people from literally hundreds of miles away, with the vast majority from many miles distant. A number there had never even been to the property.

After allowing the mob rule for a few minutes, the supervisor quieted them with another speech. "Ladies and gentlemen," he began, "it seems rather evident that we have a rather sizable opposition to the proposal." More jeers and cheers followed, with the supervisor raising his hands to continue. "In all fairness to both sides, I think we should have a town hall meeting in the Grange hall near the property in question so that everyone can have as much time as he or she desires to debate this issue." More cheers. "Is this all right with you?"

The vocal ones present let him know that it was, and then turning to me, he added, "And, Mr. Anderson, is it all right with you?"

Since our choice was that of defeat tonight or a Grange hall meeting, I nodded our consent.

"And since I am the elected servant of this fine area," he went on, "I suppose it falls on me to preside at the meeting to be sure all is fairness and right."

And he should have added—reelected.

Chapter 9

A Cornhuskin' or a Hangin'

The Grange hall was an old frame building in Welcome Valley that had probably once served as a rural schoolhouse. *Rustic* is probably the most aesthetic word that could be used to describe it.

As the board members, all of whom had decided to attend, and I drove into the parking lot (a euphemism for field), the atmosphere around the building seemed charged with feeling. In one corner stood a group of men drinking, laughing uproarously at someone's remark. Clusters of women bunched here and there, gazing in our direction and exchanging whispers. Kids raced in every direction in the carnival-like atmosphere.

Occasionally we could hear comments above the rumbling and noise, such as, "We'll get Anderson tonight." "They'll never make it." "Why do we have to put up with this?" "Wait till we get through with them."

I had some idea of how Daniel felt when he was being lowered into the den of lions, and I was thankful that my board were there with me.

A Cornhuskin' or a Hangin' 63

Not all of those present were unfriendly, however, and a few even came to wish us well. With the opposition so loud and boisterous, it was as if they were associating with untouchables.

"We're all for you," one person commented, "but it doesn't look too good. I can't decide if this is a cornhuskin' or a hangin'." Naturally, that didn't help a whole lot.

The supervisor soon arrived, and the meeting began. First we listened to another political speech concerning his wonderful benevolence and fairness, and then, turning to me, he said, "Now, Mr. Anderson, you may speak."

Quietly explaining our program and how the young people would be well supervised and trained, I spoke a little concerning our emphasis on learning a trade. The crowd seemed fairly attentive, and aside from the mumbling undercurrent, caused no outward disturbance.

"Now," the supervisor said to the mob, "I'd like to hear your objections, if there are any." As if a gate had been lifted that had held back the floodwaters, the people started yelling and shouting, with some stamping their feet. The torrents of abuse began.

"We don't want 'em here."

"Let's save our swimming hole."

"Don't want no niggers 'round here."

"That's where me and my boys hunts ever' year."

A realtor stood and claimed that it would lower the value of their property, and another "neighbor" delivered an undisguised threat to burn us out if we moved in. A few more gave some opinions that were unprintable. The tumult was unbelievable. It didn't matter that I had heard the same "reasons" before or that none of them made any sense. They wanted the use of that property whether we owned it or not.

Finally our minister, who was a member of the board, graciously stood up to speak. Before he had a chance to say half a dozen words, there came more shouts of defiance. Someone yelled, "Shut up, and sit down."

It seemed altogether too obvious that nobody could reason with the mob. Pastor Williams had just sat back down when the ex-cop accosted him. "Why don't me and you just step out back of the building," he challenged, "and we'll just settle this man to man."

More noise and illogical accusations followed. Finally a county social worker stood up to speak. I had never met him and didn't know what his position was, but the supervisor recognized him and ordered the crowd to quiet down.

He gave some statistics on juvenile crime in the county, then went on to say, "Our department is crying for schools like this. It seems to me that this boys' ranch would do our county a real service by caring for our young boys."

More boos and hisses drowned out his next statement, and he, too, sat down. (Later I learned that his speech had placed his job in real jeopardy due to pressure from the supervisor

A Cornhuskin' or a Hangin'

seeking reelection. I went to the young man's office and thanked him for making an effort in our behalf. "Well," he said to me, "I wasn't intending to say anything, but I couldn't stand to see this wrong being done.")

Then Big Ed jumped to his feet, and I knew that we were in for some real straight talk. He lived across the road from our property, had known everyone in the area for years, and was bigger and tougher than any of them, but had a heart of solid gold. First he ordered them to sit down and be quiet. And they did.

His eloquence that night was unmatched.

"You folks are unbelievable. These people have come to our area to try to help us with our problem youngsters, and you won't even listen to them. As each of you know, I'm a probation officer in this county, and I know the problems we face. A lot of you should know them, also, 'cause I've processed your kids into juvenile hall and the county jail. You're only thinking about your own selfish interests. Do you think that property belongs to you? Did you pay for it? You people ought to be ashamed of yourselves. I'm ashamed . . . to call you my neighbors."

A moment of silence followed as Big Ed sat down. And then the crowd gave a thundering ovation, but it was difficult to see—my eyes were a little misty.

The final decision would come at another hearing of the planning commission at the courthouse. The meeting adjourned.

The next few days were one letdown after another. In spite of Big Ed's persuasive speech, the old cliché held true that "a man convinced against his will is of the same opinion still." Since many of those attending the meetings had their own ulterior motives, few had changed their stance.

The morning of the last planning commission meeting I drove down to talk with a member of it who was definitely friendly to our project. Although I was quite certain what he would say, I did seek his advice. He had had to keep a low profile in his support due to his position, but he had let it be known that "as a private citizen and adjacent property owner" he was all for approving the zoning change allowing our operation and had even signed a petition to that effect.

"I guess you know why I'm here," I greeted him and sat down on the other side of his desk.

"Yes," he said, "I've been sort of expecting you. I wish I had some encouragement to give you. Carl, you know most of us in this office are all for your boys' ranch going in here. But," and he sighed sympathetically, "you don't stand a chance at that meeting. Even if by some miracle the planning commission voted with you, they can appeal the decision to the board of supervisors, and I know they would turn you down. This bunch is a minority, but they're very loud. It would be uphill all the way. Even if the decision swung your way, they'd take you to court and beat you somehow."

A Cornhuskin' or a Hangin'

I recalled the threat to my life, the vandalism that could very possibly be directed toward us, and the new rumors which had filtered in that day.

Although the disappointment was keen, I was grateful for the people who had tried to help. Thanking him, I walked down the hall to see Big Ed. He was busy at the moment, so I stopped to get a drink from the fountain beside his door and accidentally overheard him talking.

"I sure like Anderson's group," he said. "That church almost got me to join them, but I can't go along with burning in hell because I eat meat."

A pleasant female voice answered him. "That isn't what they believe. They don't look at meat as right or wrong, but simply that they'll be healthier without it. In fact, only about half of the church are vegetarians."

"Is that right? That makes sense. But I couldn't go along with any other books replacing the Bible, either."

"They don't have any books that replace the Bible," the secretary replied. "They get all their doctrines straight from the Bible."

Ed went on to describe another area of disagreement and received a short Bible study on that. His curiosity was too much. "Now wait a minute," he protested, "how come you know so much about them?"

"Well, I used to be a member of their church. And you know what? I'm going back."

And with that she walked out the door toward her office.

"If only one individual learns to know Jesus Christ better," I thought to myself, "our troubles have been worthwhile." I thanked Ed for his help, but he didn't know how much encouragement he had really been to me.

All kinds of things went through my mind as I drove back to our home beside the creek. Even though I felt certain the Lord would protect me and the property, my concern was not for myself, but for the boys, many of whom were already unwanted in their own homes. Would we really accomplish anything by placing them in another situation in which they would be unwelcome and perhaps verbally or physically abused? I knew that we really weren't left with any choice, but with this negative answer came a lot more questions that I didn't have answers for.

"I've been praying all day," Marlene said, wanting to know what had happened since I had left early that morning. "What did you find out?"

"We're going to withdraw our petition," I announced with what little courage I had left. Sitting beside the stream, I tossed in a handful of dry pine needles.

"Then we're all washed up?" Marlene asked, slumping into a chair. "No boys' ranch? Why? Why were we led to this point and now——Why?"

I didn't have an answer, just a conviction that we should withdraw our petition. The sun slipped toward the mountains. Only thin shafts of light filtered through the tall, green pines.

Marlene began cooking our last squash, and I knew that was about all she had left to cook. The staples Grandma had given us were long gone. We had a few nuts and cucumbers and the one last squash. But we both knew that the Lord would provide. "Please don't fix any for me," I told her. "I'm not too hungry. I thought I might go to the meeting a little early."

Depressed and shaken at the turn of events, I drove the twenty lonely miles to the courthouse. As I drew near, I could see that every available place was taken in the parking lot, and cars lined the streets for some distance in either direction. Not able to make myself turn in, I drove on by, around a few blocks, and again passed the courthouse. Since I didn't feel like talking to anyone before the meeting, I waited until exactly seven-thirty before parking on the street and walking to the auditorium.

I had called my board members to inform them of my decision, one that most of them had reached weeks before; so few, if any, of our supporters were present. It didn't seem to have hampered the attendance in any way, however, for people had taken every seat—in the aisles, lining the walls, and spilling out into the hall.

I excused myself through the crowd and made my way to a seat reserved for me on the front row. The anticipation and undercurrent felt at the last two meetings were even more abundant here, and this ill wind was not tempered by the love of those friendly to our position. Knowing their attitude, I would surely have feared for my life had I not come for the purpose of withdrawing our petition.

The chairman of the planning commission, with whom I had talked earlier in the day, rose to speak. "Before we start this meeting, Mr. Anderson has an announcement to make."

I stood and faced the crowded room. "We do not wish to force our way among you. Our only desire in coming here was to provide a home for boys who might otherwise not have a chance in life. Many of them come from homes where they are not wanted, and we feel we would be doing them a disservice to place them in your midst, where they are also not wanted. Therefore, Mr. Chairman, we respectfully withdraw our rezoning request." Stepping from the platform, I walked briskly toward the rear doors, the jammed aisle clearing a path for my exit.

Stunned silence rocked the room. I had expected cheers and applause, but no one breathed.

By the time I reached the rear door, the impact of my statement had begun to soak in, and the evident letdown became visible and audible. I could hear their comments to each other ringing down the hallway after me.

"I drove two hundred miles to see this fight."

"Yes, I thought we'd really see a knock-down-and-drag-out tonight."

A Cornhuskin' or a Hangin'

"Yeah, no blood or nuttin'."

Instead of going right home, I drove around trying to sort out the questions in my mind. It was after eleven o'clock when I rounded the last curve and dodged the last chuckhole in the road. The gaslight was still on, and I sensed that Marlene had been praying for me since I left.

Knowing what had happened and that I hurt too much to talk about it just yet, she kindly didn't ask any questions. What does one say after watching his dreams disintegrate in front of him?

"Sleepy?" I finally broke the silence, although I knew she wasn't.

"No," she replied.

"Let's move. We're all washed up here."

As we picked up our folding chairs, she asked, "Where will we go?"

"Oh," I said thoughtfully, "maybe Nevada. Someday I'd like to live there."

So at midnight we "folded our tents like the Arabs, and as silently stole away," leaving behind us the ashes of our hopes and dreams and a year and a half of work.

Chapter 10

Triumph or Defeat

We spent a few days in the peace and solitude of the Nevada desert and then headed back to the work that we knew had to be done.

Unfortunately, since I was so sure the Murphy Ranch was where we were supposed to be, I had neglected to place a provision in our purchase contract to void it if we were unable to get necessary permits. Our first order of business was to sell the property to recover our down payment.

For weeks I put advertisements in all the local papers and gave listings to the realtors. Mid-November found us still unable to sell the ranch, and I continued looking far and wide for a new home for our boys. The camper wasn't exactly warm. Snow would be coming to the Sierras soon. The four walls in our four-by-eight-foot camper, with its ceiling so low I couldn't stand straight, were daily getting smaller. Another flea-market sale and parting with some of the last of our antiques enabled us to arrange to move the small mobile home to a trailer park and pay the

Triumph or Defeat

first month of rent. Although we were out of money again, at least we would have a little more living space.

We drove our camper to the mobile home park and anxiously watched while the movers unhitched the trailer just as the sun slipped behind the distant hills. Unable to hook up the necessary utilities that evening, we waited expectantly for the dawn, sure that a new day would begin a new phase in our lives.

Sitting in the camper, we had a praise session for the blessings granted us. First, of course, was the trailer next to the camper that would soon have heat and electricity. Next we talked about how grateful we were for the camper, as small as it was, that had served as our home for the past four months. Then we praised the Lord for our propane tank that had not failed us. We didn't know if the small five-gallon tank was filled when we bought it or not, but we knew that for the past four months we had used it for all our cooking, hot water for dishes and an occasional "bath," and our only source of heat for the cold fall days and nights.

We slept warmly our last night in the camper and with anticipation prepared to move into our eight-by-thirty-nine-foot mobile home—not dimensions that would likely be called luxurious, unless compared with the alternative. As we finished our last camper breakfast, we sat for a moment deciding which job to tackle first. Suddenly the flame on the burners that had served our every domestic need gave a little flicker and died. Like the widow's cruse of oil in 1 Kings 17, it stopped when there was no longer a need. The Lord knew we didn't have money to refill it, and we didn't have to. It was just another of His ways of saying, "I love you."

The trailer was longer but not a lot warmer, as the oil furnace didn't work properly and the fan didn't function at all. We could turn it on only when we were right there to make sure it didn't get too hot and ignite the cabinet.

A few days after we had settled into our trailer, the snow came; and with it, subfreezing temperatures. Our kitchen faucet had an irritating drip. Every morning we woke to find an icicle from the faucet to the bottom of the sink. In less than an hour the oil heater had the little kitchen warm, and we thawed our feet and the faucet icicle. The snow fell softly and stacked on the trees and cars, with not a whisper of wind to drift the huge flakes.

But the problem with the sale of the property and location of new property still faced us. We would not give up if it took all winter and summer and then some.

Our continuing headache, of course, was money. Finally I consented to let Marlene go to work—if she could find a job. The nearby aerospace industry had just laid off several thousand employees, and the prospects were not encouraging. The employment agency announced that they had only one job opening. "But short-

Triumph or Defeat

hand is required," the woman said, closing her book sympathetically.

"But I take dictation by shorthand," Marlene put in quickly.

"You do?" she said, opening her book and proceeding to fill out a form. "This job is for a church secretary. We've sent several girls to the pastor, but we have no word that any of them have been hired." She handed Marlene the form. "Good luck."

Alone in the car, Marlene thanked the Lord for the one job available in the whole town. "If this is Your will, please impress the pastor to hire me." She breathed a sigh of relief and commitment to His will and headed up snowy streets to the church.

The minister was friendly but as nervous as the applicant. He dictated a short letter, which she read back to him. Many of the words were in longhand, and the transcription wasn't too good. She was too nervous to do a good job since it had been years since she had been forced to think in shorthand characters.

"He just smiled and asked when I could come to work," she chirped excitedly to me later. "I told him I could come tomorrow. But I really wasn't sure if he was hiring me or just asking questions. Then he said, 'How about eight o'clock tomorrow?' He said he had had an appointment with another applicant later this afternoon, but she couldn't take shorthand, so the job is mine if I wanted it."

The main pastor dictated his sermons, which were mostly on brotherly love and politics. More of the latter than the former. Often the same thing week after week, with a few illustrations here and there.

His evenings were full with youth and young-married sessions and reality therapy. Not all of the sessions were in the name of religion. He condoned "pot" and initiated in the church basement a coffeehouse that later turned into sensitivity sit-ins, or as some called them, play-ins.

His associate, a retired gentleman who wore the distinguished honorary title of doctor, talked "our language," and we had many religious discussions. His love for Jesus was undeniable.

One day he related an incident to Marlene: "I was out visiting one of our parishioners yesterday when I got stuck on the muddy Johnson road. I tried and tried to get out, and then I thought to pray. As soon as I had prayed, I tried again and drove right out."

"Doctor, isn't it wonderful how the Lord answers our prayers!" Marlene said. "Prayer is a way of life in our family too."

The young pastor broke up with laughter. "You don't mean to tell me you believe God answered your prayer? That's just fairy tales."

"I surely do believe it," replied the older man.

"I do too," Marlene put in. "He has answered many for us in our work toward a boys' ranch."

But the younger man was not convinced.

Triumph or Defeat

Marlene had many good chats with the old man, who was sincerely concerned about the spiritual changes he observed in his church. One day I asked her to take him a copy of A. Graham Maxwell's *You Can Trust the Bible*. He thanked her and began reading. From her desk she heard him exclaim, "That's right," and later, "I believe that too."

"Marlene," he called from his office, and she went in. "I've read this whole book, and I believe it." He paused, picking up his worn Bible. "You know most of the modern churches have gotten away from this dear Book, but it's the one true guide we have."

"Yes," she replied, "there's nothing that can take its place, is there?"

His face saddened. "I'm so discouraged. The trend is all toward philosophy. And prayer——?" He shook his head. "Prayer, they say, is very 'old-fashioned.' But I believe the Bible just like you do."

A few days before she left the job at the church, the kindly old man again brought up the subject of prayer and the love of God. He stood in the doorway of his office and looked intently at her, with tears in his eyes. "Marlene, I'm going to miss you. Let's meet in heaven." We've thought many times since then that if God directed all of our trials in Welcome Valley so that old gentleman could have another glimpse of heaven, it would be worth every heartache and trial we had endured.

Chapter 11

The Lead That Finally Led

The weeks of searching and trying to sell stretched into months of anxiety and strain. I followed up on dozens of leads, only to find they went nowhere. Besides the use of time and energy, it placed a heavy toll on us financially, as Marlene's salary barely paid for our trailer space, utilities, and a little food to go with our pinto beans and rice.

One day, as I was talking to Pastor Williams on the phone, he mentioned an individual who had once offered some property for a school. "I don't know," he said, "but it wouldn't hurt to check. His name is Dr. Charles Lindsay."

Thanking the pastor, I soon had the doctor on the phone and stated the purpose of my call. "It sounds interesting," he said. "Can you be at my office at twelve o'clock tomorrow?"

I left early the next morning to make sure of arriving on time, which I did—about an hour and a half early. The doctor picked up sandwiches from his home, and we headed toward his property. As we rode along I ex-

The Lead That Finally Led

plained the purposes and aims of the corporation, the need for such a facility, and my lifetime dream of a boys' ranch.

"You know, Carl," he interrupted, "I have always wanted to have a boys' ranch, but the opportunity never came. Just kept putting it off, and now I guess I'm too old to start one." His statement was familiar. Dozens of individuals in the past two years had expressed the same desire and then lamented, "Now I'm too old to do it."

"My property begins here," he said, pointing to a landmark.

Around a couple of curves and up a long driveway we passed through a gate and onto a trail that wound among giant oak trees and through gullies. He stopped his car at the edge of a large meadow. The view was breathtaking, the early wild flowers were blooming in great profusion, and Mt. Dixon rose abruptly at the far edge. Pine and oak trees surrounded the meadow with a few madrona and lots of manzanita growing under the towering trees. Several springs trickled through the meadow and then into a larger stream that babbled over rocks and fallen logs in its zigzag course. On the extreme end of the property stood a new stucco house.

"This house is on my property, all except four feet of one bedroom," the doctor explained. "It wasn't planned that way, and they wouldn't believe me when I told them, so they built it where they wanted to anyway. After it was built, they had it surveyed, and due to the fact that it wasn't on their property, they couldn't get title or utilities to it, so there it sits."

We walked through the house. Mud two or three inches thick and animal droppings covered the floors from the front door to the back. The back door was missing, the windows were boarded up, but it appeared to be a lovely, large home used only by the animals at the time.

"I'm buying the additional acreage in order to clear the title," he said. We walked through the meadow and forest as he talked on about his property, showing on a map the boundaries and the lay of the land. "Well, Carl, what do you think of it?" he turned to me.

"It's beautiful, just beautiful."

"It's yours."

"Thank you," I said. "You're an answer to our prayers."

"You're welcome. And you're an answer to my prayers. I've been struggling in my mind as to what I should do for the Lord, and for the past six months I have been praying for answers. Today I'm willing and grateful to donate the property. Six months ago, at the time you were having problems locating a place, I probably wouldn't have been interested."

I could hardly wait to get home and share the good news with Marlene.

She met me at the door. "What happened?" she asked. Before I could reply, she rambled on, "I could hardly work all day. I prayed almost constantly and kept thinking about how wonder-

The Lead That Finally Led

ful it would be if he would donate the property."

When she paused, I interjected, "He did."

"He did?" She snapped to the reality of my statement. "He donated it? No money, no strings—free? Fantastic!" Finally she relaxed. "Tell me about the place."

I described to her the ranch, the house, the possibilities. We talked for hours about the miracle dropped on us that day. Now that it had really happened, it was almost a shock to us.

The last year we had nearly become transients. After we sold the Murphy Ranch, we worked just about anywhere to enable me to continue searching for property. Consequently we had just completed our eighth move in twelve months, with at least one more move anticipated, and moving wasn't getting any easier. The last three houses we had lived in temporarily had required scrubbing and complete painting of interior and exterior. "I've never scrubbed so much in my life," Marlene moaned. "Not even doing free labor in school."

But finally, after two years of waiting, planning, sacrificing, and praying, we were within a mile of moving into the ranch house. We rented a too-small, two-bedroom cottage. It was rough, to say the least. The living-room walls were a chocolate brown and had been patched and repatched where previous tenants had started but never completed remodeling. The two bedrooms had a four-foot opening between them that didn't allow for much privacy. We hung some old curtains to divide the area into two small rooms.

Our son, Chip, was not to be lonely, however, as the first of thousands of phone calls and letters soon reached us.

"I'm sorry to bother you now," he said. "I know you aren't ready to take in boys yet, but Ken really needs some extra help right now. Would you be willing to take him?" I've always been a soft touch for a young person in need, so I told them to bring him. Chip and Ken occupied the smaller of the two rooms that opened onto the kitchen.

The large kitchen was adequate in space but had few cupboards, and the whole thing was filthy. So, once again, we started from scratch to clean and make a home for ourselves. Due to a lack of funds we agreed to paint the interior and exterior for one month of free rent.

It was unusually cold and rainy for the first of June. Every morning we had a fire in the old wood stove in one corner of the living room. I had to be gone quite a bit raising funds; so Ken, Chip, and Marlene kept the home fires burning and cared for our dog, Champ; Chip's two finches, Mr. and Mrs. Beasley; and Ken's blue jay, Dumb-dumb. That is, until the day Dumb-dumb, living up to his name, fell into his drinking water and expired.

We moved things from the rented garage as often as I went to Lodi, and before long we were relatively warm, dry, and comfortable.

The next call for help brought Tom and Alan

The Lead That Finally Led

to live with us. Since there was no place to put them except the living-room floor, Ken joined the two new boys, and all three set up their bedroom in the living room.

Although we were eager to move into the ranch house, the electricity wasn't hooked up, thus we would have had no water, no toilets, and no lights. Each time we contacted the utility company they promised, "We'll be out the end of this week or next week for sure." For four months "next week" never came.

Because of the several inches of mud and animal droppings we couldn't immediately move into the ranch house. We scooped up the buckled tile with snow shovels and took it to the dump by the pickup load. After painting the interior, we once more scrubbed—then again and again. The windows required several washings to get the film off; then we replaced the broken panes.

The house, relatively new, was well built with large rooms and plenty of storage space. For some reason it had been built on the side of a hill without any landscaping. Over the years, every time it rained, the water and mud washed in the front door, through the house, and out the back door, leaving another deposit of debris. That first winter we sandbagged the front door and built a trench around the house to allow the water to drain, but still we had problems. Eventually I was able to borrow a bulldozer to dig out some dirt, then built a retaining wall with native stone.

That solved the problem, but until then it was a real nightmare of watching the front door for telltale signs of high water seeping under the door and of ditching in the rain.

"Some folks camped in here once," said a neighbor who stopped by to say hello. "When they were here," he said, "I saw a pig walk right out this front door." We could believe it, by the condition of the house!

Little by little, the house began to look and smell like a human habitation. The floor looked better with the mud and tile gone, but as Marlene said, "Carpet would really be nice, quieter, warmer—and prohibitive."

"Not necessarily," I reminded her. "I know we can't pay cash, but we have good credit with Sears. Maybe they even have carpet on sale right now." More than once we had been thankful for good credit, and although we really didn't want to push our personal credit too far, we decided to check.

At Sears we found exactly what we wanted, but because it was such a large purchase, they checked our credit record. I knew that would not be a problem. "Only routine," they told us. In our imagination we had the carpet laid in every room and the furniture placed.

"I'm sorry; we can't extend credit," the clerk announced. "Our records show a delinquent balance."

We insisted we had paid the balance months before and that we didn't owe Sears any money.

The Lead That Finally Led

They maintained we did—and that was that.

Back at the pickup, Marlene kept saying, "There's something wrong. I just don't understand it."

"Well, we can't do anything about it. But let's stop at the carpet place on Sixteenth Street."

We told the salesman what we were looking for. He led us to a roll of carpet, the color and brand identical to the one we had chosen at Sears but nearly three dollars a yard cheaper. In addition, we got a discount because we took the whole roll, both of which enabled us to pay cash.

Incidentally, our next Sears statement showed a zero balance, so whatever their problem was, Providence was leading us to buy the same carpet at a tremendous savings.

Moving day came at last. We were going into the ranch house, finished or not, for the simple reason that we didn't have money for another month of rent. The luxuries consisted of wall-to-wall carpeting, lights that came on with the flip of a switch, and windows that opened.

However, we had our share of inconveniences to balance them, such as no pump and therefore no water or toilets, a broken window, and three frames with no window at all. But we all had beds and everyone was willing to put up with the problems until we could make repairs.

We had to carry water in all the containers we could find for drinking and scrubbing. Cooking on the range was a future dream. In the meantime, a Coleman camp stove served us well.

In spite of the inconveniences and the hard work that went along with pioneering the ranch, we occasionally took time out to go swimming, which helped fill the gap left by no water in the house, we made ice cream now and then for a special treat, and the boys enjoyed fishing in the small ponds, although they never caught anything more alive than a discarded rubber boot.

Our need for water was obvious. As soon as possible I hired a local well driller. Someone had drilled a well near the house some years before, but since we had no idea how deep it was or how much water was available, I asked the driller to clean out all the debris that had collected in it. The bottom was visible twenty feet down.

He set up his rig over the hole and started bringing up bucket after bucket of dirt. "Nope, ain't no water in that well; never has been," Mr. Becker stated with determination as he wiped the perspiration from his brow.

There just had to be water. Here we were trying to start a boys' ranch (we already had four boys), and God had answered so many prayers before—one being the property that was donated—surely God wouldn't let us down now.

"How deep did you go?" I asked, seating myself on the back of Mr. Becker's well rig.

"I've cleaned it out down to thirty-four feet. Most of the wells around here are about that deep. The bucket won't go down any farther. I banged it over and over again. That well has never been deeper than thirty-four feet, and

The Lead That Finally Led

there ain't no water in it." He secured the cable on the bucket. "Why don't you just drill a new well? You have to have water."

We knew how important water was. Even in early summer it can get pretty warm in northern California. But the fact still remained that we had no money for a new well.

Ken looked at Mrs. A without uttering a word, but his eyes flashed a dozen questions—questions we all felt.

Mr. Becker pulled a faded red handkerchief from his hip pocket and rubbed it briskly over his heavy growth of whiskers. "Lunchtime!" he announced. "I'll come back after lunch and move my rig. That well's never been deeper than thirty-four feet, and there ain't no water in it." He shuffled off toward his old green pickup and left in a cloud of dust.

We stood there quietly for a moment. Nobody said a word, nobody made a move—we just stared at the thirty-four-foot dry hole. I turned and walked slowly toward the car, the boys followed, and Marlene went to find four-year-old Chip, who was chasing lizards.

"Mother, is there water?" He came running, clutching a lizard in his hand.

"No, Honey, not yet, but God knows we need water. Has He ever failed us yet?"

Chip was quite grown up for his four years and had witnessed many answers to prayers. "No, He hasn't failed us." He hesitated thoughtfully, "God has always answered our prayers, 'cept sometimes it takes longer."

Back in the house Marlene prepared a quick lunch. Surprisingly, no one seemed hungry. The boys didn't tease and scuffle as usual, and little Chip sat quietly waiting for lunch.

As we bowed our heads I prayed, thanking God for the food and for His leading toward the establishment of this school. Then we laid it all before Him. "We want to do Thy will, but it seems that Old Scratch is working overtime to stop things. Lord, I pray that You will somehow give us a well with good water and plenty of it. Thank You for hearing our prayer. Amen."

Amens echoed around the table and our appetites revived as we ate lunch and talked about everything else but Mr. Becker and the well.

We were waiting at the well when Mr. Becker's pickup bumped around the curve and came to a stop by his rig, sending a cloud of dust toward us. He didn't drive fast, but the ground was so dry and powdery that the slightest movement created a dust cloud. Just one more reason why we needed water and lots of it.

"I'll drop the bucket once more. Won't do any good—but won't do no harm, either." He prepared to lower the bucket that hung by a cable from his rig.

Silently we all prayed. The boys and Chip stood quietly watching the whole operation. Mr. Becker's truck was an old army vehicle equipped with a big hoist and a pulley on the back. Slowly he turned the handle that lowered the bucket. It

The Lead That Finally Led

missed the hole, and he cranked the cable slightly to free the bucket from the edge of the well. The bucket swung back and forth slowly. At just the precise moment he quickly released the lever, and the bucket sailed to the bottom of the well.

There was a loud bang as it hit the thirty-four-foot bottom and then a swish as the bucket seemed to keep going. His eyes widened, his jaw dropped. The pulley continued to unwind the cable. The end of the cable unwound, slipped off the pulley, and dropped into the well. Mr. Becker still stood there, shocked by what had happened . . . not even aware that his bucket and all of his cable lay at the bottom of the well—eighty-four feet down—until it was all over.

Suddenly, the reality of it all hit us. Mr. Becker let out a string of oaths, and the boys whooped and hollered, "We're gonna have water!"

"Praise the Lord. He did it again."

Mr. Becker shook his head. "That was lucky."

"Actually, Mr. Becker," I explained, "it wasn't luck. It was an answer to our prayers."

He probably wouldn't have believed it except for the fact that his equipment was down in the bottom of the hole. He got another cable with a hook on the end and fished until he hooked the first cable and brought it to the surface. As his old pickup roared up the dusty road he was still shaking his head. Then he turned to wave to us as we stood around the miracle well.

Chapter 12

Fire in the Night

The summer passed all too quickly, and with September came the start of school. Lodi Academy, my alma mater, was discarding some of its old school desks and had offered them to us. A few days before classes would begin I left Marlene with the boys, who now numbered six, and drove our pickup down to get the desks. While in town I asked my grandmother if she would like to go back with me and spend a few days.

Soon we were on our way back to the ranch with the load of school desks.

Grandma and I reminisced about when she and my family both lived around Sacramento. "My, things have changed." She looked for old landmarks. "I wonder if our persimmon orchard is gone from Florin Road?" I remembered those delicious persimmons.

We had a grand time recalling the times when we boys were young. By the time we had traveled some thirty miles from Lodi, but were still eighty miles from the ranch, the engine developed a persistent knock that I couldn't ignore. Pulling

Fire in the Night

into a nearby Arco station, I waited for the mechanic to confirm my diagnosis. "I'm sorry to have to tell you this," he apologized, "but your motor is just worn out. That knock is the main bearing that went out."

I sank three steps lower in my spirits. Why did it have to happen now? If I had been alone, I wouldn't have cared so much, but what was I going to do with my eighty-year-old grandmother? "Lord," I prayed silently, "I know You have a plan in this somewhere even if I can't see it now, so I'll just lay the burden on You." Then I felt better—but not a lot.

"It will take me about a week to make the repairs on the engine," the mechanic said. "Do you have someone who can come and get you?"

"No, our other car had a hole in the gas tank, so I brought it along to get it repaired. Marlene doesn't have transportation either."

"If you can wait a few minutes till I close up, I'll take you home," the attendant volunteered.

"Well, I wasn't going anyplace, anyway," I laughed. "But that's a long way for you to drive."

"Don't mind," he countered. "Besides, how would you get home?"

He had a real selling point there. In a few minutes we were on our way to the ranch, tired, but not defeated. However, we had neglected to get the gas tank, so I still couldn't fix the other car. The realization hit Marlene the next morning. "Hey, we're without transportation."

"Right," was my unenthusiastic reply. "I got

the gas tank repaired, but it's still in the pickup."

She had no real choice but to call the dentist and cancel Chip's appointment for that afternoon. Our dentist was one of a kind and, suspecting a problem, asked why she had to cancel. Briefly she told him about our car problems. He said he'd be right over with their family's second car. "Keep it as long as you need it," he said.

The Good Samaritans of this world were still around—first, the Arco attendant and then our dentist.

With David, Denny, and John having recently joined our ranch family, our need for a school was becoming acute. A friend offered the free use of a house about a mile from the ranch, which we gratefully accepted. Now all we had to do was to get our pickup with its load of desks, and we would be ready for school.

We enjoyed Grandma's visit. She loved young people and the adventure of the project. When the station finally called to let me know the pickup was ready, she was busy in the kitchen. The bill he quoted was way beyond our budget, however. The engine had needed a complete overhaul with many additional replacement parts.

"Don't worry about it," Grandma consoled. "I can see that you are doing a good work. I'll take care of the bill." Grandma was always there when we needed her. Her small income didn't go far, but with frugality she was able to save for projects like the truck repairs.

Fire in the Night

We all crowded into our dentist's car the next day to take Grandma home and get the pickup on the way back. The trip was uneventful, and we arrived home about an hour before sundown. Marlene and I were tired but happy. The boys, however, wanted to start school immediately.

"No," I told them, "it's too late in the day, and the electricity hasn't been turned on yet. We'll start in the morning, but if you want to, we can go set up the desks and get the room all ready."

Their yells and screams were evidence enough of their eagerness to get school underway, so we dusted and cleaned and put everything in order. It was amazing to see the enthusiasm of those boys who had "hated school" previously. In a few minutes we had cleaned the house, set the desks in order, and even hung a few charts and pictures. Someone suggested it had been a long time since lunch, so we locked the building and got into the pickup.

Since darkness was setting in, we decided to take the short route that led through the upper meadow, along the creek, and through the forest instead of the four-mile route by the main road. Before we had gone far, Dirk jumped out of the pickup and bounded off across the meadow in an effort to beat us home. The cow trail that we followed in the pickup led over washes and ravines and a thousand chuckholes, and by the time we reached home, there was Dirk, huffing and puffing, but looking pleased with himself.

It had been a wonderful day, and sleep came easy. We had the gas tank for the car, our pickup was running and the bill was paid, and our school was cleaned, set up, and ready for classes the next day. After a day of such accomplishments, we slept well.

At 11:30 the phone awakened us. I answered sleepily. It was the doctor. "Someone just called and said the school was on fire. See what you can do."

Stunned, then shocked, I replied, "We'll be right there. Thanks," and I hung up.

I yelled to the boys to get up. Marlene, having overheard the conversation, gathered Chip along with his blanket and pillow. "Get the shovels," I shouted to one boy. "Get all the garden hoses . . . and the pick." The boys ran here and there getting the tools.

Quickly we were in the pickup, heading through the forest, along the creek, and through the upper meadow toward the school. We drove about sixty miles an hour, and our prayers for our school were even faster. The chuckholes leveled out, and we literally flew over the ravines. Finally we rounded the last bend, and our hearts sank.

Our beloved schoolhouse was nothing but smoldering ashes about eighteen inches high. A few neighbors stood around quietly talking, and a sheriff's deputy stood off to one side. Marlene started to cry, and my eyes weren't too dry either. Reluctantly I went over to the deputy. "Do you know how it started?" I asked.

Fire in the Night

"Yes," he said, "it was arson. I know who did it, but I'll probably never be able to prove it. Two men were seen near here after dark. There's only one thing I can't figure out. What are all those steel frames in there?"

"I know," I replied, "those were part of a dream."

A saddened group drove slowly back through the meadow and along the stream, but the beauty was hidden in the darkness.

The next morning we sadly returned to the site of the former schoolhouse, unable to comprehend the tragedy. A little smoke still puffed here and there, but the two stone chimneys were all that stood more than a few inches above the ground.

"Now we'll probably all have to go home," one boy sniffed.

"No, we won't," another corrected. "We won't have to leave, no matter what happens."

"Maybe God wanted it this way," someone suggested. We all agreed that even though this temporary location seemed suitable, maybe God had better plans for our school.

Although we had lost one house by fire, our friend kindly offered the use of another. Other friends soon located more school desks for us, which we set up in the log house not far from the site of our first school. We decorated the rustic living room with maps, charts, and other school things. School went well in the log house for about two weeks . . . until the county building inspector found out we were holding classes there.

"You'll have to put up fire walls and fire doors and a sprinkler system or . . . move out," he told us.

The fire protection improvements he suggested were absolutely out of the question, so we folded our maps, packed our books, and moved to the ranch house living room. Two days later we had a phone call. "I was wondering if you would like to have a small mobile home? It's free, but you will have to go pick it up. It could serve as a temporary school."

"Yes," I replied, "we would be happy to pick up the trailer." Soon our boys had a new school in the thirty-five-foot trailer, which served us well for several months until we were wall to wall with school desks—and more students coming.

Everyone knew about our school fire and the temporary trailer that we had outgrown, but a longtime friend, whom we affectionately called Aunt Sadie, got busy and did something. First, she located a new modular classroom for sale, then she made arrangements for an abandoned building that the owner had consented to let her use rent free. There she set up shop for a first-class rummage sale.

Sadie solicited salable items from every source in Lodi and the surrounding area that she could think of. The newspaper carried advertising, the radio station had spot announcements, and the rummage came in by the truckload. If

Fire in the Night

something needed mending, Sadie did it. Items Sadie couldn't repair, her handyman husband could. Soon several other women and some men volunteered to help sort and sell items. They donated their time week after week.

Merchandise flooded the building, but so did the shoppers. "This isn't a rummage sale," one person commented; "it's a department store." And it did resemble one, with things neatly organized and displayed.

Sadie ran the sale for a month and then a few extra weeks because the response was so good. But finally, exhausted, she felt that she just had to call a halt. However, since so many regular customers begged her to continue the sale a little longer, she relented and kept the doors open two more weeks.

Aunt Sadie never failed to tell her many customers that the proceeds were going to buy a school for the boys' ranch. Her long hours and hard work, as well as the time spent by her helpers, resulted in over six thousand dollars, which paid to move the new classroom and purchased another steel frame that ultimately became our cafeteria. She launched and successfully completed several other fund-raising projects, also, including one in which a group of friends from the church I had attended most of my life bought a dishwasher and gave it in memory of my mother.

Others took their cue from her success, and soon Granny Thelma had organized another successful rummage sale in Placerville. Then the Brooks family in Modesto said, "Give us a list of things you need." We would have hesitated to do such a bold thing, but we knew the Brookses well. Since they insisted, we complied, and they launched a campaign to obtain what we needed. The Lord blessed their efforts, enabling them to supply most of our items on the long list—even a lifetime "want," when some friends donated a Hammond organ.

I'm constantly reminded of Matthew 6:33: "Seek ye first the kingdom of God, and his righteousness; and all these things shall be added unto you." The organ was not an absolute necessity, but it provided a lot of pleasure and enjoyment for the staff and students. We've found that often the Lord impresses someone to give a few "wants" along with our "needs." It's nice sometimes to have a little frosting on the cake. Fire had destroyed one dream so that we might have bigger and better things.

Chapter 13

Safe in a Boxcar

"You aren't going to move in boxcars, are you? They will be an eyesore." Being president of the board, he was naturally concerned about such things. "No, I don't like that."

"What do we do then?" I asked. "We can't afford a barn, and we're desperate for room. Follow me," I said, leading the way into the house. He hadn't been beyond the living room . . . not until now.

In the dining room I pointed to the corner. "See those barrels? That one has bedding in it; this one, extra clothes. This one says 'food.' Probably powdered milk, beans, and extra flour," I conjectured. "These boxes are filled with canned fruit we brought with us, and some we canned last week."

He poked his head around the other side of the barrels. "What?" he gasped. "You have boys sleeping here."

"Have to," I replied. "The barrels, boxes, and extra refrigerator serve as a partition so they can have some privacy." I called his attention to the desk behind him. "That is where Marlene does the bookkeeping and correspondence. She says it seems so silly to knock on a barrel before she goes to her desk."

"Man, can't you put some of this stuff in the garage?" he asked. "This is terrible." I opened the garage door to reveal hay and oats, saddles, our antique square grand piano, paint, nails, garden tools, and hoses.

His mouth dropped.

Maybe I had a case after all. "One of the boxcars I looked at has a wire-cage toolroom on one end," I continued. "The other end is floor-to-ceiling cubbyholes for nails, paint, plumbing supplies, and that sort of thing." I thought I detected some sort of consent in the man's eyes. "The other boxcar has a door on one end. I figured we could use it for a tack room and the saddles and for stacking the hay. We'll get everything out of the garage, fix it up, and move some boys out there." He didn't comment.

Taking him to Chip's room, which my son shared with David, I opened the closet door. "These are boxes of food Pathfinder Clubs around the state donated. Without their generous help, we would have gone hungry. Some clubs give half of the food they collect at Halloween to the Indians and half to us."

"I see," he nodded.

"Of course you realize feeding this many boys takes a lot of food."

"It won't last long," he agreed.

"We have boys sleeping everywhere except in our bedroom and the bathroom."

He grinned and suggested we not go that far.

"Good news," I continued. "My dear little grandmother gave the money for one boxcar. Naturally she'd prefer that my family use part of it for personal storage, like the end opposite the tack room." He stood silently, staring at the floor. "Are you still with me?" I prodded.

"Ye-s-s," he drawled thoughtfully. "You've convinced me. I'll buy the other one."

"Thanks a million," I exclaimed. "I already have ten-foot, tongue-and-groove plywood for a high fence around the boxcars. We'll put redwood stain on the fence."

"That ought to hide a multitude of sins."

"It's too bad you don't have time to see the barn we have our things stored in. The barn is five miles away, so we have to stack the things here at the house that we need each day, plus things like the piano that we are trying to keep away from mice and rats."

He nodded. "I'm sure that would be an experience all its own, but I've got to get back to town." I thanked him for his time, and he drove away.

When we left our lovely home in Lodi to move to the ranch, we stored everything we owned, except for a few clothes and essential cooking utensils, in a rented garage. "We don't have to spend a great deal of time stacking the boxes in an orderly fashion," I suggested to Marlene.

"We'll be moving out in a few months."

Those few months ran into a year and a half. The garage rent was reasonable, but ranch funds were limited, and my salary was something we only talked about and hoped for. Somehow the small gifts we received, added to the antique sales we had periodically, saw us through. In fact, our antique collections, as often as not, paid for ranch improvements, utilities, or ranch gas.

But to avoid more rent, we moved our furniture and personal belongings to an old barn we had received permission to use. It was in no way secure, but having it close, we could sort the stuff, get out our winter clothes we had managed to survive without the previous winter, and maybe with some of our antique treasures pay a few more bills.

Grandma Seltmann, Marlene's mother, came to visit the day after we moved the last of our things from the garage. Through her motivation and insistence, she and Marlene went to the barn to sort our belongings. "This is just some of my clothes," Marlene commented as she pushed a box aside.

"Wait a minute," her mother protested. "Let's have a look." She opened the box. "Did you wear this last year?" she asked, holding up a dress.

"Well, no. It was packed."

"Did you wear it the year before?"

"What is this, 'Twenty Questions' or 'I've Got a Secret'?" Marlene asked, but she knew her mother was right. "Actually, it's been a couple of years since I've worn it."

"Then it's time to get rid of it. Isn't there someplace you could take used clothes?"

"Yes, there is. Let's start a box. I have a feeling there will be a bundle.

"Oh, no. This is the box I dumped my dresser drawers into when we moved." Marlene moaned and slammed the lid.

"I know it's painful, but let's get at it." Grandma Seltmann sighed. "If I didn't suffer through this stuff with you, when would you do it?"

"Never!" came my wife's quick reply.

So they sorted hour after long, hot hour and ended up with mounds of clothes and boxes of junk and trash. Then they took our good china and silver to the ranch house along with a carload of immediate needs.

"Carl, we brought most things of real value to us except the hall tree and your rocks." Marlene looked tired. "There is so much left, but we really don't have any place to put it here."

Trying to console her, I said, "Someday we'll have a place to put it. The boxcars will be here soon. Until then, we'll just do the best we can."

Saturday night we always planned games and something special. This particular night we decided to run over to the barn and get a box of funny old hats so the boys could play musical hats. When I saw the barn, my heart sank. "I'm afraid we've had company. The door is open. It's been kicked in; look, the hinges are off." We groped around with the flashlight, trying to see what was missing.

"Hey, they took those boxes of clothes . . . and the trash too." Marlene had things stacked and knew where everything was. She made a quick trip around the barn.

"Saved you a trip to town," I soothed.

"There is stuff missing, but I really can't see well enough with this light." She strained to see labels on the boxes. "Your trunk is open."

"Yes," I noted sadly, "and our tennis rackets, balls, mitts, sleeping bags . . . they're all gone." I closed the lid.

"What about your rocks?" Marlene started jerking open the drawers in my antique dental cabinet. I joined her. The drawers were empty. "They surely were thorough, weren't they? That's sickening."

"The Brazilian agate is gone," I moaned, "and the petrified palm. Have you found the little plastic case with the heart in it?" It contained a rare heart-shaped agate with a crystal in it. "Maybe I should have sold it when I had the opportunity. What about the box of large crystals?"

"They were right here." She hurried to open a box. "They're gone."

We prayed a great deal that night that somehow, someplace, we would find the things, especially the heart agate and crystals and the halltree mirror.

Early the next morning we returned to the barn with mixed feelings, wanting to find our treasures but not wanting to face the loss.

"Fantastic," I suddenly shouted, barely believing it was true. "Here's the mirror for the hall tree. They must have intended to take it but forgot." I beamed as I picked it up. Could it be? "Look, Honey. Here are my crystals . . . and the heart agate." I held it so the crystal caught the morning sunlight. "Isn't it beautiful? They moved these things over to the door to take them and apparently forgot for some reason."

"I didn't fare so well," Marlene spoke sadly. "They took my little china cupboard. It was so dear to me. Grandpa made it, a replica of Grandmother's."

"I'm sorry, Babe." I tried to console her. "No doubt it was that little china cupboard that inspired you to collect saltshakers as your grandmother did." I straightened. "What about your saltshakers?"

"Oh, dear." She ran to a corner. "One, two, three, four . . . and there's the barrel. Well, I still have them," she sighed with relief. "Let's take them home with us and all of your rocks too."

"We'll take all we can," I replied. "Some of this stuff no one would want."

How wrong I was.

The next Friday we went back to the barn and filled the pickup with treasures, antiques, and junk to take to the flea market in San Jose. Although it was many miles over there, the sale was large, and we always found it worth our time and expense to go there to sell anything and everything.

Because of the distance, we left Saturday night, planning to sleep in the pickup so as to be there bright and early. Fifteen minutes down the road, I pulled over to the side and stopped.

"What did you forget?" Marlene asked.

"Nothing," I replied and sat there a few seconds. "I just feel we aren't supposed to go to the flea market." Turning around, we went back home.

Early Sunday morning we unloaded the pickup and went back to the barn for another load. We needn't have bothered. The thieves had been there some time after we left Friday afternoon and had taken several twin-size mattresses, some glassware, and more antiques.

"They took my bassinet," Marlene wailed, "the one all us kids slept in."

I stood shaking my head. "I can't believe it. Last week they emptied my wooden trunk; this week they took it."

"And the old beat-up green file," Marlene laughed.

"You mean the wooden one with the big hole in the side?"

She nodded.

"Boy, they are desperate. What about the stuff in the drawers?"

"There wasn't much, just scratch paper and magazine pictures," she replied. "I took all of the music last week when I took the stories and poems."

"Let's move everything today." I started hauling boxes to the pickup.

Marlene sat down on a bench. "Why, oh, why haven't the boxcars come?" She put her head in her hands. "Every time it dries out enough to call the movers, it rains again. Look how much stuff we've lost. Why?"

"I can't say, Babe. Maybe we have something to learn." Cautiously I added, "It hurts when we lose things with sentimental value, but they won't be important to us in eternity."

"I know," she sobbed. "But what about the old school bell, the trumpet, and candlesticks? They were valuable, and we were going to sell them. Every dime we've gotten from sales has gone into the ranch."

"That's true," I had to admit.

"How long has it been since any of us have had anything new or had a dime just to waste? We've given everything, and now this . . ."

"Well," I said, trying to console her, "I don't have too many answers, and I, also, have a lot of questions, but I'm sure God will bless us if we just stick in there. He never promised that it was going to be easy."

"I know," she said, drying her eyes. "I'm all right. Sometimes I forget."

In a few days the boxcars were in place and served satisfactorily for many years until we erected a new steel barn.

Chapter 14

Blessings Always Boomerang

The miracles seemed to come as fast as we could handle them. One after another, doors opened that had been closed tightly. Steve and Ben soon joined us, and as our ranch family grew, the expenses soared. Besides living expenses, we needed funds for building and repairs, insurance, and a hundred other things. In the meantime, we did all we could with what we had.

From the back of the house to the creek was not more than six hundred feet, but manzanita brush effectively blocked the pathway through what otherwise would have been a continuation of the meadow. Old, with a lot of it dead, the brush came out fairly easy. Evenings, after working on the house and a cottage for more boys, we built a bonfire and tried to make a game out of pulling out the brush by hand and throwing it on the fire. Due to the fact that there is probably a little of the arsonist in all of us, it made a difficult job a little easier.

Uncle Cliff had joined us as house parent in

the cottage, and the progress increased correspondingly. He owned a pickup with a cable winch on the front. Thus we were able to dig the larger manzanita, but it took a long time.

"Carl," Cliff said one evening as Marlene struggled to pull a manzanita tree too big for her, "we really need a caterpillar with a hydraulic blade. We could do as much work in one hour as we all do in a month."

I had to agree with him. "I'd be happy to have anything on wheels or skids." A caterpillar-type tractor seemed the best way to save a great deal of time and energy, but finances being what they were, it was out of the question. In fact, at the time of this writing, some twelve years later, we still don't have a "cat," so we continue to clear brush the hard, time-consuming way. But we keep hoping . . . someday.

Soon the rains came, and the need for a cat dropped off the highest priority list except for each time we got stuck in the mud. It then zoomed back to the top of the list.

One day a tall, slightly balding man visited the ranch and noticed our need. "Could you use a tractor?" he asked, scanning our small array of tools and equipment. "It's an old orange, rubber-tired tractor, Allis Chalmers, I guess. In fact, we've had it for sale for over a year without a single bite."

"We would surely put it to good use," I quickly assured him. I could envision moving logs, grubbing brush, pulling cars out of the mud, and plowing the garden.

"You may have it," he said, "although there's no hurry in picking it up. I don't suppose you really need it until spring."

Thanking him, I assured him again that we would indeed come and get it. Days and weeks turned into months. We remained busy with speaking engagements, running here and there, and school.

"I made arrangements to pick up a refrigerator and quilts in town Thursday," Marlene announced one day. "They have some boxes of 'miscellaneous items,' probably food and clothes. Those ladies have really been great."

"Fine," I replied. "I can take some of the boys to town in the afternoon and get it."

Thursday morning, however, when I awoke, I knew I had to get the tractor that day. There wasn't any voice; I just simply knew. "Honey," I said, approaching her in the kitchen, "I'm going to pick up the tractor today."

"Today?" she looked at me in disbelief. "You've got to be kidding. It's been raining for weeks. It will be a month and a half before we will need it for the garden. Besides, I told the lady we'd get the refrigerator today."

"Well, the boys can go with you and get those things," I reasoned. "But I've got to get the tractor today." I knew she still wasn't convinced, but she took the boys, and I went after the tractor.

We both returned home about the same time and looked over our new treasures. Then the

Blessings Always Boomerang   111

phone rang. "Carl, it's a miracle," the former owner of the tractor exclaimed. "I've seen a miracle. I just can't believe it." He took an excited breath and hurried on. "Just after you left, a man drove into my yard and wanted to buy it, and he had the cash in his pocket. I didn't even know the guy. I've tried to sell it for a year with no success. And you know what?" He chuckled. "If he had beat you here, I'd have sold it. But I'm so glad you have it now."

"Now I understand your urgency," Marlene smiled. "He leads in mysterious ways, doesn't He?"

Our little Austin automobile, which we had nicknamed Jitney, got smaller and smaller as new boys arrived. By now the little car was pretty crowded. We had been praying for someone to donate a vehicle, and as Jitney choked and sputtered along, we prayed even harder.

One day a doctor and his wife came to see the ranch. I took them for a tour in our little Austin, and the sick little piece of machinery hardly made it up the two-foot incline in the driveway to the main road. She had taken me many thousands of miles in the past two years over rough roads, freeways, and cow trails, but this would probably be her last tour.

Our guests got quite a ride over the one hundred acres. After we returned to the ranch house, the doctor commented, "Carl, you need a car that runs better than the one you have. We have a Volvo station wagon that we would be happy to donate."

Two days later Jitney refused to be coaxed up the driveway again. In fact, we had to crank her to get her running. The following day she was pretty sick, and we feared she would expire right there in front of the house. Fortunately that was the day I was to meet the doctor and get the Volvo. How grateful we were for it, and it served our needs quite adequately . . . more space, and it ran better. But thousands of miles later we began having problems with the car. Although we repaired one thing, two more went wrong.

Then one day we got into the Volvo, which the boys had renamed Vege-buggy, and went through the usual procedure: coast from the top of the hill (where we purposely parked it) beyond the driveway to the parking lot, past the gate and the house and all the other familiar landmarks, on through the big gate, over the culvert to the bridge at the bottom of the hill to where the road started up again . . . but this time it stubbornly refused to start. With the many thousands of miles we had added to its already overdone odometer, it was just worn out. Since we had long ago outgrown the Volvo, we put a vehicle on our list of things to pray for at worship—a larger vehicle, one that would accommodate all of us . . . comfortably.

One day on our way home from an afternoon youth activities appointment, our car again refused to cooperate. In fact, our friends had to pull us to get it started so we could even leave town.

Blessings Always Boomerang

Naturally we prayed that the Lord would guide and protect us and keep the Volvo running till we reached home.

Little red Vege-buggy sputtered and choked over first one hill and then another, around curve after curve. Each time we prayed it would keep on going. But, alas, twelve miles from the ranch, it stalled and refused to start. As always, we took the problem to the Lord, asking that He work a miracle and somehow get our tired old car running and us home.

The engine still refused to start. It seemed the only way we would make it home was for me to catch a ride and ask a friend to come pick up the rest of our ranch family. The sun had set behind the coastal range, and darkness settled fast that winter evening as I tried to hitch a ride. Cars just weren't stopping. After some time, one finally did.

When the car pulled back onto the road, one of the boys in the back seat of Vege-buggy exclaimed excitedly, "Know what happened?" He wiggled to get himself comfortable in the too-crowded back seat. "Just before that last car came, I prayed that the very next car would pick up Mr. A, and you know, it did!"

They talked about the answer to a boy's prayer. "But why didn't God make our car run till we got home?" someone asked. Marlene didn't have any answers—she only had questions.

They sang every chorus and hymn they could think of to pass the time and then waited in the dark. It was getting cold too. Hours seemed to pass before I returned in our neighbor's pickup with a most wonderful story—the ultimate answer to our prayers . . . a miracle. I had obtained a ride to our driveway and walked in to find the Baileys, old friends, from Lodi, who owned a nursery. "Where is everybody?" they immediately inquired.

Briefly I told them about our car breaking down and its condition. "Well, Carl," Mr. Bailey said, "what you need is a van."

I couldn't have agreed more.

And he went on, "I think I have one I could let you have."

The Econoline served us faithfully for many more thousands of miles until there came a time when we outgrew it too. We were grateful for the van, but it shrank with each new boy. If we all went, the fourteen of us packed in like sardines.

A friend watched us squeeze in one day. "Do you have a can opener?" he teased.

"Boys, we really need a bus for transportation," I announced at council meeting one night. "We're going to pray about it."

A few days later I had the impression to have a parking place made for the bus. "We must have some place to park it," I told my wife.

Several boys watched curiously as I measured and pounded stakes. "Mr. A, what are you doing?"

"I'm measuring a place to park the bus," I replied.

Blessings Always Boomerang

"He knows where we're going to get a bus," somebody said. They got into a huddle. All I could hear were whispers. Then the spokesman for the group asked bravely, "Where are we going to get a bus?"

"I don't have any idea. But I want to be ready. We've been praying for it, so we better find a place to park it."

Half a dozen little boys with hands thrust deep in their pockets walked on down the road kicking rocks and shaking their heads in disbelief.

A few days later we took the boys to a large west coast youth seminar that they had looked forward to for weeks. The side door of the van opened, and boys began to file, and fall, out. A woman stood nearby watching the seemingly endless stream of boys. "Mr. Anderson," she exclaimed, "you need a bus."

"You're right, we do," I replied, adding that we had so many needs we just couldn't afford one.

"Why don't you let me see what I can do?" she said. Within a few weeks we had a Greyhound silver-sided bus.

Excited about the answer to their prayers, the boys kept inquiring, "What color is it? How big is it?"

We only answered, "Time will tell."

It was long after dark before we arrived. The boys had gone to bed but were by no means asleep. As I rounded the corner I saw them standing at the cottage window, noses pressed against the glass. When I blew the air horn, the cottage erupted as pajama-clad boys danced from every door, waving their arms and shouting. I opened the bus door before it had even come to a complete stop. They climbed aboard, ran straight to the rear, and leaned back in the seats. Their ride continued . . . all the way to the parking space we had made for the bus.

"I've been praying for a bus," one boy announced, "but I didn't expect the Lord to send one like this. Now I have to believe in prayer."

The bus faithfully served our need of transportation for our boys, but I still needed a small car for use for publicity trips and speaking engagements. A physician acquaintance called one day to say that he had seen our notice in our monthly newsletter about an economy car. I assured him that it was something we really had to have. "Now I know why I haven't been able to sell my Volkswagen," he said. "I've had it advertised at a reasonable price for the past several weeks and haven't even had any offers. You may pick it up whenever you're ready."

I thanked him for his gift, and in a short time we doubled the mileage on it. The story doesn't end there, however. "Due to the gift exemption, I came out about the same financially, without the headache of selling," he said later. "And," he added, "it did a lot of good for the ranch besides."

Since that first car, he has given numerous

others and found that on late model cars he did better on his tax deduction to our nonprofit corporation than he would have had he sold them outright or traded them in on new ones.

Chapter 15

Death Gives Way to Victory

Paralyzed with fear, I held the razor to my face and waited for the scream that I felt would come. I hadn't been to her room, and no one had told me, but an inexpressible feeling came over me with the message, "Be prepared."

Marlene paused at the door of the bathroom, where I was shaving, and calmly remarked as she did every morning, "I'm going to check on Angela."

I just knew something was wrong.

We had always had a lot of boys in our family. My wife and I each have three brothers and no sisters, our cousins are nearly all boys, and our foster children had been mostly boys. The one thing we needed to make our family complete was a little girl.

Thus we had been to an adoption agency and left our name with several doctors. The latter weren't too helpful, saying they hadn't had many babies for adoption in a long time. The agency was even less encouraging. But we filled out the application anyway, and more months went by.

Death Gives Way to Victory

After several years of waiting we talked it over and decided there was no point in keeping all the baby clothes and furniture around any longer. "Let's give them to someone who can use them. We've stored them long enough," I urged. Although we knew it was the thing to do, our hearts still yearned for a baby girl.

The next morning Marlene stacked the boxes of baby things in the living room and picked out some of Chip's baby clothes she wanted to keep. However, before she finished, Dr. Lee phoned. "Are you still interested in adopting a baby girl?" I could hardly believe it was true, but Dr. Lee wasn't the type of person to phone long-distance just to make a joke.

Immediately we planned for the trip, anxious, excited, and very grateful. The Lord had worked it out at just the right time.

We encountered a few delays on the trip, such as blowouts and flat tires, but the bright spot was the excitement over naming the new baby. The list of names lengthened, then we narrowed it down. Finally we settled on Angela Lou. It had special significance, for we felt that God had sent us an "angel," and Lou is Marlene's middle name.

Angela was a week old when we first saw her. The doctor's family had cared for her for a few days until we arrived. Mrs. Lee smiled when we told her we wanted to name the baby Angela. "That's interesting," she said. "We've been calling her Angel." And she looked like an angel, so tiny and feminine.

On the way home Marlene reached over and touched my arm several times. "Honey, I just can't believe it. Am I dreaming?"

"No, it's for real," I smiled. "It surely is an answer to our prayers."

All the way home the motion of the car kept Angela sleeping. When we arrived at 6:00 AM, it was time for her feeding. From that day on, she slept all night every night.

A baby in the house after six years didn't really demand too many adjustments. She rarely cried and seemed to be happy wherever she was. We took her wherever we went. Friends always remarked that she was a beautiful baby.

We dedicated Angela to the Lord when she was three weeks old. The Lord had given her to us, and we felt the dedication to be an important part of her life.

Angela matched the visions one has of little curly-haired cherubs, and she seemed to grow larger and healthier every day. The smiles and chuckles she willingly gave seemed to dissipate problems. Each periodic checkup assured us of her normal growth and development. Her three-month physical was scheduled for Thursday morning.

Wednesday morning as we sat eating breakfast, I felt a strange compulsion that Angela should go to the doctor that day. When I mentioned it to Marlene, she readily agreed, and I dialed his office.

Death Gives Way to Victory

The receptionist answered, and I came right to the point. "My wife has an appointment for our baby tomorrow. She's due for her checkup, but I was wondering if she might be able to come in today instead."

"Is the baby sick? The appointment is scheduled for 10:00 tomorrow."

"No," I replied. "She seems to be healthy, but I was wondering if you might have an opening today?" Checking the doctor's schedule, she confirmed an appointment for Angela at 1:30 that afternoon.

Marlene arrived a little before the scheduled appointment, and the physician and nurses seemed to enjoy a few extra minutes with Angela, who cooed and gurgled to her appreciative audience. The examination was soon completed. Dr. Swenson beamed as he pronounced her "growing well" and in "excellent health."

In spite of the good report, I stood there the following morning with a heavy premonition of tragedy. My wife walked into the nursery, and unmistakable feelings of anxiety and uncertainty swept over her. Without even glancing at Angela, she hurriedly retraced her steps, pleading with me as she passed the door, "Will you check on her, please?"

Without bothering to wipe the lather from my face I slowly placed the razor on the edge of the sink and took the dozen heavy steps to her bedside. As I uncovered her tiny body, the impact of our tragedy forced me to my knees. Never have I experienced such deep pain or hurt so intensely. I thought that I would surely lose my mind. It began to pound and turn. I couldn't understand why it had happened to us. Slowly I returned to thoughts of the rest of my family, and I shuffled to the kitchen, where Marlene waited.

No words were needed to explain.

After a few moments of uncontrollable grief, Marlene pleaded, "Let's pray." As we poured out our hearts to the One who is still in control, He came close, and I recalled the words of Matthew 5:4, Deuteronomy 31:6, and 1 Corinthians 15:52: "Blessed are they that mourn: for they shall be comforted." "Be strong and of a good courage, fear not; . . . he will not fail thee, nor forsake thee." "For the trumpet shall sound, and the dead shall be raised incorruptible, and we shall be changed."

My mind went back to the church service a few days before when I had sung the Bill Gaither song "Because He Lives." When I came to the second verse, I changed it slightly to fit our home: "How sweet to hold our newborn baby, and feel the pride and joy she gives." The song goes on to describe the love of parenthood. But more than anything else and regardless of the future, we need not be afraid, "because He (Jesus) lives." A flood of peace swept over us as we remembered.

Though God had come near, and the hurt was beginning to lessen, life still seemed empty and cruel. The morning had hardly started when

Death Gives Way to Victory

six-year-old Chip awakened. Before we could explain our tragedy, he began to relate a dream he had about "sorrow and women crying." When we told him of our loss, he said through tears, "I think God let her die because He's coming back real soon. This way she won't have to go through the problems."

A few minutes later a young couple drove into our yard. The only words they spoke were, "I'm sorry," but that was enough. Though I had employed them only weeks before, they had come to mean much to us. They understood, for just a short year before they had also lost someone—their only son—to infant death syndrome. They knew what real empathy was.

The God who takes care of our needs, in addition to His presence, gave us that day a son with reasoning beyond his years, friends who truly understood our grief, and the peace of mind to know we had done our best.

In spite of the pain and loss of this trial, we thanked God for the three precious months with our "angel." And though her death has left our family incomplete for now, it has made heaven so much dearer.

Chapter 16

"Give, . . . and It Shall Be Given"

Problems mounted, but the Lord had an answer for each one, even if it was at the end of our own arms. It seems He never does things for us that we can do for ourselves. Our financial needs were, are, and probably always will be one of the most acute and pressing dilemmas.

The board had voted a salary for me at the very beginning, but the first three years we didn't receive a regular salary because there just wasn't money. I had hoped to be able to repay myself for the thousands of dollars of personal money I had put in over the years, without even thinking about a salary, but my hopes were growing dim. Now we had to have a septic system and needed money to pay for it. We had prayed that when the job was finished, the money would be there, but in fact, it wasn't. I talked it over with the contractor.

"Well," the man suggested, "I could use a pickup. Would you be interested in trading yours for a septic system?"

The pickup belonged to me personally, and

"Give, . . . and It Shall Be Given"

we really needed it. My personal car, Jitney, had long since given up, and I dreaded the thought of being without a car of my own. But since we also had to pay for the septic system, I made the swap.

The students knew of my deal and told new kids, who repeated it to the next batch. Several generations of boys later, a little freckle-faced rancher came up to me and asked, "Mr. A, is your pickup 'for really' in the septic tank?"

God knew of our need and didn't leave the ranch without a pickup for long. One morning while Marlene typed and pasted a newsletter together, she asked, "Do you think we should ask for a pickup in it this month?"

"Well," I replied, "I think it might be a good . . ." The phone rang, and I went to answer it.

"Guess who called?" I teased a few minutes later, but she had no idea where to begin guessing since we received so many calls every day.

"It must have been good; you look like the cat that got the goldfish."

"That, my dear, was Mr. West, and ——"

"You know," she interrupted, "every time I think about him, I remember his confidence and the first thousand dollars toward your dream. What did he want?"

"Well, he hasn't forgotten us, and he was just wondering when I could come down . . . and get a pickup he has for us."

"You don't mean it!" She jumped up from her chair. "We didn't even have to ask. That's sort of like Daniel—while he was yet praying, his prayer was answered."

Many of our other friends were sacrificing in addition to the Wests.

Mrs. Evans had been interested in the ranch from the start and eagerly helped with or totally sponsored various projects. Though she was an elderly widow living on Social Security, she insisted on contributing.

"Carl"—she had approached me one day in her businesslike manner—"I'm going to sell my little house. I should be able to get twelve thousand dollars for it. If I can get that much, I'll give the ranch a thousand dollars."

"That's wonderful, Mrs. Evans," I said. "Will you list it with a realtor?"

"Oh, no. I don't want to pay any commission."

Eager to assist, I inquired, "Could I help you write an ad for the paper?"

"No," she replied quickly. "I'll just put up a sign."

"I could put one up out by the street," I said, picturing a four-by-eight-foot sign attracting prospective buyers.

"No, I was thinking about putting a small sign in my window."

I even volunteered to go to the dime store and buy one, but she wasn't as excited as I was.

"Thank you, anyway," she said kindly. "I'll go to town one day this week."

Although I wondered to myself if she really wanted to sell her house, I told the boys about

"Give, . . . and It Shall Be Given"

Mrs. Evans' house and her generous gift. We prayed that the Lord would sell her house—and added—"for the right price."

She did buy a small sign and put it in a window. Two days later she was out watering her roses when a man walked by. Seeing the sign, he called, "Hello there, your house for sale?"

"Yes."

"May I see it?"

"Surely," she responded and showed him through her house.

Back at the door he inquired, "How much are you asking?"

Mrs Evans did some quick mental calculating. "I needed room to dicker," she explained to me later, "so I told him I was asking fourteen thousand dollars."

"That's too much," he said, looking around the living room. "I'll give you thirteen thousand dollars cash."

"I'll take it," she replied. Just that fast her faith was rewarded, and the thousand dollars she pledged to the ranch was made up to her so that she ended up with her original price.

Fund raising never was my favorite responsibility, but I've knocked on so many doors and held down waiting-room chairs at such lengths that if they gave parking tickets in waiting rooms, I would have had plenty.

Often the response was, "Well, I'm broke, but I've got this fantastic idea whereby you can make a 'killing.'" To mention only a few, they included the stock market; raising frogs for restaurants, chinchillas for fur, dogs and pigs for research, even fishworms; hatching queen bees; selling firewood, mistletoe, and pinecones; making jewelry of stones; cutting records; painting and sculpturing; writing books; giving concerts.

We considered a few of the ideas but felt we could not spend the time and work involved. Small boys would be of little help and then only under constant supervision. The facts were we didn't have any extra "supervisory" help. Thus we felt that we had to put our priorities with the boys and their needs and trust God to provide the means.

At one time we desperately needed five hundred dollars to pay bills that were due. Unfortunately we didn't have the money, nor were we expecting it. Consequently we made our need a matter of prayer. Monthly donations were small, although regular, but we couldn't wait several months to pay these particular bills. Working with our students, I couldn't take time off to go raise the money . . . so we continued to pray.

One day in the mail we received a letter from Pastor Fenton, a missionary in Taiwan, halfway around the world. His note read, "I feel impressed that you need this money and that you need it right now. Enclosed please find my check for five hundred dollars."

When he returned to the States, I asked him about it. "I had been praying for the ranch," he

"Give, . . . and It Shall Be Given"   129

replied, "and had a very distinct impression that you needed money. I told Ruth I was going to send you our savings. She asked how much I intended to send, and I replied, 'All of it,' and she said, 'Okay.' "

I visited various people, some with money, some with small pensions. Their reactions were interesting and varied.

"Why don't you see Mr. Lamson," someone suggested. "He's a pillar in the church and owns a very prosperous business in town." So with a prayer for the Holy Spirit's presence and guidance, I went to see Mr. Lamson.

"No, Carl," he said, "to have a home for these children would only be cause for more problem boys."

"I don't understand," I told him.

"Well, the reason children have problems is that mothers work. If you take care of their children, more mothers will work."

It was rather ironic that he had several dozen mothers working for him at that particular time.

Another family I had known for some time seemed interested in the project. "We're sorry, Carl," Mrs. Young said after a while. "We're so poor, I just don't know how we're going to live. You know Jim is facing retirement in a few months, and I don't know how we will make it." My eyes glanced around the room adorned with antiques and exquisite imports. In fact, it was the first time I had ever been in their plush living room. Usually we visited in the family room or the garden room. "We might be able to scrape up ten dollars. We really believe in what you are doing."

When I related the incident to Marlene, she was concerned, but only passively. "Maybe we should send them a food basket."

Two days later they left for a two-month tour of Australia and Asia. "Guess we're too late for the food basket," I laughed.

It didn't bother me that they went on several tours each year. In fact, I'd like to travel more than I do, but their pleas of poverty were somewhat disconcerting.

In another case I presented a rather wealthy couple with our needs. They listened, then he leaned back in his chair and chuckled. "Well, my wife and I have worked hard, and what we have, we've earned. Frankly, we plan to spend it and enjoy it."

I told him I appreciated his honesty. What he did with his wealth was up to him and God.

Another excuse I got was, "We're going to give our money to help work right here in our own area. We don't want it to go beyond our community. That is where we earned it, and that is where we want to spend it."

That, too, was an honest reply, and I feel that worthy home projects should receive first priority. I could have reminded them that our school serves a need that is not and cannot be met in the local community.

Another man had just retired. "I'm really

poor, Carl," he told me. "Retirement isn't what you might think it is." The next day he went out and paid cash for a lovely new car. A few weeks later I visited him in the hospital. "Well, Carl," he said through his pain, "I do have a little cash socked away." I hadn't mentioned money and had come only to express my get-well wishes. "But," he continued, "I'm going to spend it on myself. Do a few things, buy a few things. Just sort of enjoy my retirement years." He was talking honestly, but three weeks later I attended his funeral.

A retired minister once met me with, "Don't bother me about it; I'm not interested." In later years I got the feeling he rather regretted his decision, for whenever we met, he greeted me with, "Well, Carl, my boy, how is your good work coming along?"

On one of those trips when I had a deadline to meet, one professional man said, "I don't have much to spare right now. I'll give you one hundred dollars, but if you don't get all you need, let me know." The Lord blessed my further contact, but the man donated again on other occasions.

A personal friend moaned, "Carl, things are really bad. The new business isn't prospering like it used to. We haven't even had money to pay tithe."

I knew him well and could talk to him straight, and I did. About tithing mostly. Reminding him of God's promise in Malachi 3:8-10 to "pour out a blessing, that there shall not be room enough to receive it" if we are faithful in our tithes and offerings, I encouraged him to "prove" it for himself as Scripture tells us to do.

A few months later I met him on the street. "Say, Carl," he beamed, "stop by my office sometime. I have something for you." As I stepped into his office later he handed me a check for five hundred dollars and said, "I'm paying my tithe, and you know, our business is just booming."

I knew Mrs. Daniels was poor in material goods. She didn't fare too well in the marital department either. Her husband opposed everything she did and let her know it in no uncertain terms. Consequently I purposely avoided asking her for money because I knew she had to scrape for her grocery dollars. But she sent a letter with ten dollars and a little note: "How I wish it could be more." What a joy it is to meet with those who have given and sacrificed that one more boy could have a chance to know Jesus Christ.

One of my all-time favorite people is a little jewel of a lady in her eightieth year who is so full of love for the less fortunate that each month she sends several dollars out of the hundred-dollar pension she has to live on. With the encouragement and love of people like that, our work still goes on.

Chapter 17

Help!

Over the years we have had a real potpourri of staff members. As a rule of thumb, we observed two distinct classes of personnel: those who could get a job anywhere and loved working with the boys, and those who couldn't get a job anywhere else. One of our best was also our first employee.

Cliff was a short little man with bowed legs that matched his ready smile. If he didn't know how to do something already, he'd figure it out. Not only could he work with new materials, as we all prefer to do, he was a master with the used, bent, and broken, and if he didn't have a part, he'd make it.

People often wrote and said we could have some leftover parts, tools, or building materials, which—due to our financial condition—we were, and are, thrilled to receive. We sorted through each box and were often surprised to find just the thing we needed for a special project we were working on. Many times the Lord impressed someone to give a tool, a hose clamp, electrical material, lumber, or something else at exactly the time we needed it.

Cliff helped us build the cottage and became the houseparent to ten boys. When the cottage became too small, we received a double-wide trailer to house additional boys. He moved over to care for them. For the cottage we then hired a single woman as housemother for our younger boys.

In time a romance developed, and "Uncle Cliff" and "Aunt Mary" set a wedding date. Our boys felt all along that they had had a definite part in the match and could hardly wait for the day. They were more nervous than the bride and groom. One would have thought they were the ones getting married.

Finally the time arrived, and each boy put on his best clothes and behavior. Karl, being the tallest of the boys, had the honor of escorting Aunt Mary down the aisle. Marlene was the matron of honor; and I, the best man and soloist. The guests were mostly boys.

The wedding went smoothly until the minister came to the point in the ceremony where he said, "Who giveth this woman to be wed to this man?" He was not quite prepared for what followed, as all of the boys jumped to their feet and shouted, "We do!"

The rest of the service was anticlimactic.

We appreciated their help as well as that of so many other wonderful workers.

John was one staff member who, although a

good worker, was also rather accident prone. He got along well with the students and other staff, but he always seemed to be waiting for an accident to happen. Who else could cut his foot open while waterskiing in the middle of a lake? Who else would back into the only power pole anywhere near our swimming hole?

Nor has anyone else ever backed the van over the edge of the parking lot and required prayer and a neighbor's tractor to keep it from tipping over. And then there was the time he was riding on the back of another staff member's truck when it hit a bump. He flew into the air, did a double flip, and landed on his head in the ditch. Fortunately, he didn't get hurt, for which we were truly grateful.

And his next week wasn't that terrific either.

Linda, our cook, was having a birthday, and John wanted to do something especially nice for her. While she was in town shopping for groceries, he decided to make her a cake. He mixed the ingredients and baked the cake, which turned out just about perfect. It wasn't until he was finishing the chocolate frosting that he really ran into problems. As John cleaned the electric mixer, still running, with his index finger the inevitable happened. It pulled his finger between the blades and took the tip of his finger right off. Bleeding profusely, John wrapped the finger in a towel and went to find someone to take him to the doctor.

A while later, one of the boys, not known for

his cooking abilities, saw the red "food coloring" in the chocolate icing and proceeded to finish the stirring job that John had started. Another helpful staff member noticed that John had not been able to finish icing the cake and promptly completed the job.

At supper that night everyone enjoyed the cake except one boy who had helped in the kitchen all afternoon and "wasn't particularly hungry for cake that night." Suddenly another boy let out a shriek as he pulled something from his cake. "Oh, yuck," he gasped, "a fingernail." The boy who "wasn't hungry" then burst into uncontrollable laughter and told what had actually happened. After everyone, holding his stomach, had run for the outdoors, a lot of kids wanted a real old-fashioned "tar and featherin'."

Carney was another staff member who was so good natured we couldn't help but like him. He wanted to work at the ranch so badly that he said he would gladly do just about anything. When we told him we needed someone to do the laundry, he quickly volunteered. As it turned out, Carney was interested in a particular young woman who worked at the ranch, and his mind was mostly on her. But, as Marlene said, "How can anyone possibly goof up the laundry?"

We didn't have to wait long to find out.

First it was the socks. Carney, thinking he would "even things out," gave each boy five pairs, regardless of the name on the socks. Then there was the time he put any sock with any other

Help!

one. "'Cause nobody sees the kids anyway." Or the wool coats that he washed in hot water or the white shirts he washed with the blue Levi's . . . which were bleached. And then there was the time he called from the laundromat thirty miles away and left word to say, "Since I'm already in town, I'm going to run on up to see my brother." His brother was four hundred miles away in Portland, and the boys weren't too happy to have to wait a week to get their laundry back.

Next, I thought I would try him on the woodcutting, as we always needed a lot to keep our fireplace going. "Mr. Carney," I asked, "have you ever used a chain saw?"

"Yes," he replied, "I'm quite familiar with a chain saw. What do you need cut?"

I showed him a tree to cut up for firewood. While I figured that he could use a chain saw, I didn't realize that he didn't know how to fell a tree. But he went to work in earnest.

"Timber," he yelled, and the tree started coming down right where he stood. Fortunately he ran in the other direction, and the tree missed him. But unfortunately, he had parked the pickup in the wrong place. The tree hit the pickup, then rolled around until it effectively blocked his retreat. He cut up the tree so he could drive out. Since the damage to the pickup was minor, he was able to back the pickup and trailer over a huge boulder, which effectively wrecked the trailer.

"Could you change a flat on the VW?" I asked

him one morning.

"I'm sorry," he replied, "I have a dental appointment at 11:00."

Thanking him anyway, I went to fix the flat myself. Carney left for town early, and I thought no more about his appointment until he returned to the ranch about six thirty that evening. One of the boys asked curiously, "What did the dentist do?"

He frowned and scratched his head. "That's what I went to town for! I kept wondering all day why I went."

Since he loved to go to town, I decided I would take advantage of that. "I think I'll send Mr. Carney to the airport to get Jim," I told Marlene. "I don't really feel like driving the four-hour round trip to the airport after teaching all day."

"No reason why he couldn't do that," Marlene laughed, "as long as he doesn't take bleach and wool coats."

Mr. Carney showed his usual degree of eagerness. I handed him a note with Jim's airline, flight number, and time of arrival. "Leave in plenty of time so you're there when his plane arrives," I advised him. "It will make the boy feel good to know that someone is there to meet him."

That night I was musing to myself about how nice it was to have someone pick up the boys at the airport, when the phone rang at eleven thirty. "This is United Airlines. We have a Jim Stephens waiting for a ride. He gave me your number. Our terminal closes at 12:20. Will someone be here to get him? He's been waiting since 6:55 this evening."

I told him I'd be there as soon as I could, but it would take me at least two hours. Jumping in my car, I dashed to the airport, worried that Carney had had an accident. The terminal was closed when I reached it, but someone had kindly waited with Jim. As we left with Jim's luggage, who was crossing the street but Mr. Carney. I blinked and looked again. "What happened to you?"

"Oh," he laughed nervously, "I got here a half hour early, so I went back to my car for a little nap. Guess I overslept."

I should have known better, but a few days later someone had to take some of the boys to an orchard to pick apples. The apples were free for picking, and on our meager budget we were always eager to take advantage of "freebies." Everyone was busy except Mr. Carney, so finally I decided to send the older, more responsible boys with him to pick the apples.

About an hour after he left, the phone rang. It was Terry. "I'm at a Douglas station. Mr. Carney stopped to get gas, and we all went to the bathroom. When I came out, he was gone and hasn't come back."

Since there was no guarantee that Mr. Carney would ever miss the boy, I told him, "I'll be right there," got his address, and drove the fifty miles to pick him up.

"We kept telling Mr. Carney that Terry wasn't with us," one of the boys later said. "But he just said, 'Oh' and kept going."

"Yeah," another agreed, "we told him a bunch of times. I don't think he heard us."

Another faithful employee spent weeks painting a new sign large enough for motorists to read from the highway. Finally the grand unveiling took place, and we all read in letters nearly two feet high, "Mr. A's Boys' Ranch and *Scoolh*."

From time to time people would come to paint the buildings, and visitors and staff would have a field day changing the appearance of the ranch. One particular man, billed as a "professional painter" and having some extra paint, volunteered to redo the main ranch house. I had an appointment in town that day. Returning, I found the entire house—walls, doors, and ceiling—was the same shade of yellow. When I walked through the rooms, I found that everything was yellow. Parts of the windows and carpet were even yellow. Some of the windows had been open, and the screens were yellow. My closet door had been left ajar, and I had a yellow stripe down the front of my bass viol. Even Marlene was beginning to look yellow.

"I hope you don't get yellow jaundice," I whispered, trying to cheer her up, "or we would never be able to find you."

She laughed and said, "I think he must have painted the tract house we once lived in."

Help!

Life was sometimes frustrating but never dull.

Fortunately we had many other staff members who gave excellent service—some for a few months; others for many years. To tell all the good things they did would take an entire book. Carroll and Shirley not only spent a number of years with us at the boys' ranch but helped us establish additional schools for youth.

So many wonderful people came to the ranch to help us we couldn't begin to name them. Others, unable to come, sent someone in their place or funds so that we could hire help to do the job. When a need was present, a person soon arrived to fill it.

At times a particular job required a specific expertise that none of us possessed. A car or truck would pull in, and the driver would say, "I don't know why I'm here, but I believe the Lord has sent me." No one had told the person to come—he had just felt "impressed." Invariably, after the visitor had looked around the ranch, he would see the job that required his special talents. Or we would have an opening in our staff, and someone would show up the same day to fill it.

Often they were individuals I had never met but who had been referred to us by a friend, or had read about this work, or somebody had told them about our boys' ranch.

Besides being a blessing to our students, many of them have found that they have gained new insight into the really important things in life. Countless times the staff have felt that they have received a bigger blessing than the boys they came to help.

Chapter 18

Joy and Grief

We had nearly given up hope of having a daughter in our family when a friend called to ask if we were still interested. It had been nearly three years since we lost Angela. Overjoyed, I told him, "Very definitely," and made arrangements to pay the hospital and doctor bills and pick up our new daughter.

Ruth Marie, named after our mothers, held our hearts and a certain amount of our time. Chip was thrilled to baby-sit with his little sister, however, so she presented little interference with our schedules. She grew quickly, the months passed rapidly, and we felt secure.

The ranch had added new boys and staff at the start of the school year, but we still had a need for a full-time cook. The first semester was nearly over, and Christmas vacation would start the next day, when in drove a friend I had met in Texas several years previously. Larry went right to the point. "We've come to help you." Turning to the woman standing beside him, he said, "I want you to meet Myrtle, my new wife."

I wasn't especially surprised, as Larry and his first wife had been having marital problems when I had visited in their home.

"And these are our children," Myrtle said, "Jodi, Mary, Gertrude, and Jerrie." Four attractive little girls slipped shyly out of the car.

"Myrtle's a terrific cook, if you need any help in the kitchen," Larry suggested.

"Well," I said a little hesitantly, "we do need a full-time cook."

"I'll be right there," she said and strode purposefully down toward the dining room.

No sooner had I shown Larry where he could put his things, when into my office marched three frustrated female employees. "What was that you sent us?" they demanded to know. "Some gal we've never seen before marches into the kitchen and starts telling everybody what to do."

"What's more," another put in, "she throws out Bible quotes like they were brickbats of piety."

"She does come on a little strong," I had to agree, but suggested, "We do need a cook, and you've each said we should get someone with a strong personality. Besides, we've been praying for a cook, and she just might be the answer."

The first one was not convinced. "If she's the answer, I hate to think back as to what the question was."

The third individual spoke up for the first

Joy and Grief

time. "For my part, I can put up with anybody, if it means I'll get out of the kitchen. I'm so far behind in my housekeeping that by the time I catch up I'm that far behind again."

Everybody laughed but had to agree with her. They decided to give Myrtle a chance and all the help they could.

The following morning brought vacation. Most of the boys returned to their homes for the two-week Christmas vacation, leaving just the staff and a few students to cook for. The meals were quite adequate but had not appreciably changed as was usually the case with new cooks. I encountered my three-person female army once again. "How is it going?" I asked.

"Well," one said, "we still have to do all the main cooking. She only wants to make those 'special' desserts we've been having. In fact, she's just no help at all and still orders us all around, then complains that it isn't done right."

"And her theology isn't any better, either," the next continued. "Do you know she is telling everybody that probation on earth will close this April 15 and that Christ is coming next October 15?"

I assured them I had heard her say this and was perplexed as to what step to take next. Thankfully, the students were on vacation at the moment. "I believe the problem will iron itself out," I told them. A few days later it did in a most unexpected way.

After spending the day in town buying

groceries and doing the laundry, Marlene and I drove into the ranch yard to find it buzzing with excitement. It seemed the sheriff, a juvenile probation officer, and the father of the four girls paid an unscheduled visit to the ranch. Myrtle had been arrested and was in jail, the four girls were on their way home with their father, and Larry was somewhere in the hills, where he had run when he saw the sheriff's car approaching.

"The girls were placed in the custody of their father by the court," the sheriff explained, "and when Myrtle took the girls out for a few hours on her visit, she never bothered to return them. Legally, she is still married to the children's father, as their divorce is not yet final."

In a few days the authorities let Myrtle out of jail, and she and Larry left for parts unknown. A few years later I ran into them in another state and asked her what had become of her prediction for Christ's return on October 15.

"Oh," she insisted, "I was exactly right as to the prophetic time. I was only off in the event."

"What was the event?"

"That's a secret. It was only revealed to me, and I can't tell anyone."

The last I heard of them they seemed to be doing "very well" after having started their own religion in the Midwest. The problems they had started for us were just beginning, however, and one fell on top of another.

A youth ranch in an eastern state had been having managerial problems. The ranch folk had

Joy and Grief

asked me to fly out at their expense and meet with their board, which I had agreed to do. The day before I was due to leave, I received a call from my attorney.

"You better get out of town for a few days," he said. "I have just received word that Ruthie's natural mother is in town and wants her baby. Apparently she's changed her mind about signing the final adoption papers. I've checked the papers that the doctor said had all been signed, and I find that they were not. We'll fight it through, and we still have a chance."

I sank into a chair, emotionally exhausted. A chance! Quickly I told Marlene what he had said, and she was heartbroken. If the mother showed up with a court order, we would have no alternative but to hand the baby over. We needed some time for our attorney to prepare as well as to decide what our response would be. Hurriedly we gathered a few clothes together and headed for the airport eighty miles away. From there we flew to my father's home in southern California. Leaving Marlene, Chip, and Ruthie, I caught the early morning flight to the east to keep my appointment with the other youth ranch board.

"So many loose ends," I thought. "Can it get any worse?"

I found out it could—and did!

After spending a few days advising the board as to the shortcomings, failures, and potentials of their ranch, I flew back to Sacramento, where I picked up my car and drove to the ranch, totally unprepared for the shock that awaited me.

The ranch looked deserted, but soon Jeanne, the assistant manager's wife, came out of her apartment, visibly shaken. "About an hour ago," she related, "we had another unscheduled visit from Myrtle's police friends. This time, however, the juvenile probation officer was accompanied by the building inspector and the health official. The building inspector said to be in his office Monday morning, or you'll be in jail by Friday night."

"What on earth is wrong?" I asked, aghast.

"The trailer mostly. Also, Sandy took the staff and kids on a pack trip, and they didn't clean too well before they left. The inspector wasn't real happy about that either."

After a short personal inspection of the buildings and grounds I could see what she meant. The garbage cans, full and overflowing, should have been taken to the dump, dirty clothes and dirt littered the boys' rooms, beds were unmade, the bathrooms were unclean, and paper littered the grounds.

Sandy and Jeanne had been with us nearly three years, the most valuable employees we had ever had. They were good with the kids and staff. As a rule they were most careful to follow my rule of cleaning everything before they left the ranch, "as if we expected visitors." But they planned this camping trip at the last minute, I found, and he had neglected to check the rooms.

The trailer, we knew, was in poor shape and

had several leaks. Feeling that the wiring was not safe, we had rewired it, putting the new wire in metal conduit. The old, unconnected wiring, not yet removed, had especially upset the inspector, as he assumed that it was still in use. Had other things been in order, we could have satisfactorily clarified the wiring situation, but now it fell on deaf ears. The next Monday I also explained to him that our board had met within the last month and voted to replace the trailer. I didn't tell him, however, that we were completely without funds to do so.

He informed me that he would give me two weeks to make the corrections after I received a letter specifying the problems. Then I phoned a friend in the health department who had a list of the improvements needed. Almost miraculously we made them even before I received the letter. A subsequent inspection produced smiles instead of threats.

Most of the changes involved little in the way of funds but a lot in the way of work. The trailer was the exception.

Marlene, Chip, and Ruthie had flown back to be at Ruthie's court hearing a few days after the first inspection tour. As we waited for the hearing to start we were pleasantly surprised to see our longtime friends Virgil and Cleo walk in. The couple used the boys' ranch motto, "Whenever you need us, we're here to help." They had physically helped us build the school, and when Angela died, they were there. Now here they were again.

Virgil came over and humbly said, "We have some money in the bank we had been saving for our retirement, but we talked it over and decided to put it to a use we really believe in. I want you to go pick out a new double-wide mobile home, and we'll take care of it."

Unless you've been in a similar situation, you can't imagine the burden that rolled off my back. The pieces of the ranch puzzle were falling into place. We had ventured out in faith, and God had honored our trust.

Our personal affairs were not so fortunate. After two hearings, the judge awarded custody of six-month-old Ruthie to her natural mother. No restitution was ever made to us for hospital expenses, doctor bills, or six months of loving care. And how does one place a value on a broken heart? It seemed the judge and juvenile probation officer were "well acquainted" with our work through our "friend" Myrtle.

Someone asked if we would try again with Ruthie if we could go back and start over, knowing the problems we would face. I could only reply, "Those six months were a real joy."

Chapter 19

It's a Boys' World

The boys come in a steady stream from a wide variety of homes in nearly every state and many foreign countries. Most are from broken homes, and some of them that aren't probably should have been. Each boy has a boundless energy source, leading to involvement in more than his share of unapproved pillow fights, pranks, and mischief. But more than anything else, each boy has a need to know Jesus Christ as his personal Saviour.

Some of the boys had never dressed up in a suit or been inside a church. It is no wonder that less than suitable attire sometimes creeps into the church.

One morning I sat relaxed in church, watching the boys file in and take their places. Suddenly my curiosity was aroused by an unfamiliar, out-of-place clump-clump. Looking out of the corner of my eye, I spotted Sam shuffling down the center aisle in his green rubber rain boots. When I cornered him later, he logically explained, "I couldn't find my good shoes."

If they couldn't immediately find their church clothes, they often didn't look hard and wore whatever they could grab at the last minute. Sometimes that was a patched—or unpatched—pair of Levi's, a buttonless pair of slacks, or a T-shirt under a sport coat. We did our best, and somehow, I'm sure, the Lord understood.

Another day Jeff's dirty tennis shoes swinging in the aisle attracted my attention, but my eyes did a double take. Those flesh-colored socks were real flesh. But he, too, had an explanation. "I couldn't find my socks."

"Couldn't you have borrowed a pair?"

"Dunno," he answered, shrugging. "I never thought of that."

We met all kinds of arguments from the boys, but the people at church often remarked, "Your boys always look nice." Perhaps the changes in manners and deportment mean a whole lot more than a few pieces of clothing after all.

The financial rewards of youth ranching are pretty small, but other rewards are priceless and many. Who could forget Will with a terrible habit of spilling his milk at least once a day, and some days, every meal? We put him on "glass ban," which meant that he had only half a glass at a time, figuring we would have less to clean up that way. One day he asked another boy, "John, would you please pour my half glass? I'm afraid I'll spill it." John started to and spilled the

It's a Boys' World

whole pitcher.

And there was Chris, who finally got his turn at milking. One morning I went to check on him and found him sitting beside our Holstein cow, squirting milk into his mouth. "Man, that's good stuff," he said as he wiped a stray squirt from his cheek. It was an exciting, new experience for him.

And unforgettable Steve, the one-of-a-kind, chubby, jolly, giggly boy, whose radar found every mud puddle on the ranch. His excuses were many and varied. He might giggle, "I got pushed," "It was deeper than it looked," or "Man, suddenly, there I was." None of them were convincing, and he knew it.

Marlene remembers looking out the kitchen window toward the meadow where the boys were playing football. Things didn't look quite right; so she blinked, then made a circular wipe on the windowpane just to make sure nothing was impairing her vision. "I saw fifteen figures hiking, passing, running," she said later. "They all looked the same—covered with mud from head to toe, identical except for size. And there was their coach, all six-foot-two inches of him, covered with mud, just like the boys."

She had a ready solution for the wet, muddy clothes. We hosed ourselves off outside and got rid of most of the mud, but she couldn't get a promise out of any of us not to do it again.

Boys come to us with a wide variety of problems: chronic fighting, being withdrawn, lacking motivation, enuresis (bed-wetting), dishonesty, soiling, ten-year-old thumb-sucking, or any other bad habits boys might have. Usually our efforts succeed. Once in a while they don't.

Jason, a lively freckle-faced redhead, came as a chronic bed wetter. He cared deeply and tried hard to quit, so we acquired an electronic bed-wetting pad for his bed. It had a supersensitive buzzer to wake up heavy sleepers at the time of accident. Often it eventually breaks the habit. A not-so-practical joker rewired Jason's pad so that in the night Jason received a 110-volt "shocking" message. He soon realized complete cure in spite of the "revolting" situation but probably not because of it.

Little Gary had a slight environmental speech problem and successfully tortured the King's English much to our amazement and amusement.

"You ozzies win me and I ozzies loses," he'd say.

"Always," someone tried to correct his grammar.

"That's what I said, ozzies and ozzies. Ob'iously I don't play so good, else you wouldn't ozzies win me."

"Switcherland," he said, "was high mountains. Intense is where Indians live." And once he heard the story of "Snow White and the Seven Divorce." But best of all was when he asked the blessing on our food at mealtime and prayed, "And please bless the hands that repaired it."

And then there was intrepid Tuff. We called

It's a Boys' World

him Tuff for two reasons. First, we already had a Mike at the ranch, and second, he exhibited surprising brawn for his size, picturesquely four-by-four, give or take a few inches either way. Getting used to ranch life left visible evidences of adjustment in cuts, bruises, and scabs. But through the rigors of learning to ride horses and making laps around the house in the dark as punishment for house-roughing, Tuff remained tough.

One sunny autumn morning we saw a different side of Tuff. He sat on his bed looking out the window and saw a blue jay circle an oak, then dart down and knock a small Junco to the ground. Thereupon the jay proceeded to peck out the eyes of the smaller bird, and it died.

Tuff knelt beside the dead bird. With a stick he laboriously dug a small hole in the hard dirt and buried the bird. Clearing a large area around the little grave, he decorated it with an orange flicker feather and erected a grave marker on which he inscribed in green ink his epitaph to the bird: "It was a good bird."

Harold's sunken, dark eyes were hard to erase from one's mind. He possessed a good mind but had nullified any abilities with several years of drunken and drugged orgies. When he came to us at fourteen, his wealthy parents were only concerned that he not be around boys who used "naughty" words. When he left, he had smiling eyes, a body that had lost its sallow, yellow tinge, and a real desire to make something of himself so that, as he told us, "I can help other kids that have the problems I did."

Alan, a boy with many problems, came to me just before he returned home to live. "I just couldn't leave without making something right with you. Do you remember that broken window about six months ago? I broke it, and I'm sorry." A number of years later it was my special privilege to welcome him back to the ranch as a staff member.

Lovable little five-year-old Patrick had a lot to learn, since up to the time he came to the ranch he basically "raised" himself. He learned quickly to tie his shoes. It took a little longer to get them on the right feet, but he succeeded. Another thing we drilled him about was not to hit girls.

One evening he announced to his housemother, "Suzie hit me first, only I finally 'membered not to hit her." When he paused, his housemother breathed a grateful sigh that Patrick had learned the lesson well. But he continued, "Good thing I 'membered, 'cause I missed her anyway."

His mispronunciation kept us in smiles. "If a tonic bomb hit Sampramcisco, it would blow it to tangerines."

One day I was working in the shop when Patrick came running in. He stood around for a few minutes with his hands thrust deep in his pockets and eyes staring at the floor as he paced back and forth.

"What's on your mind this morning, Pat-

It's a Boys' World

rick?" I asked.

"Well," he looked up at me and grinned, "I was wondering if I could call you Daddy like Chip does?"

"Sure," I replied and tousled his curly hair. "You call me Daddy if you want to . . . Son."

"Whoopee," he shouted, racing from the shop to join his friends.

Certain phonetic sounds were sheer torture. The *th* sound always came out like an *f*. At the table one night he started to take his first bite but stopped abruptly and stared at his thumb, which looked like he had stuck it in a bucket of grease. "My, my," he exclaimed, holding it for everyone to see, "just look at fat filfy fumb."

Perhaps what one of our little boys said as he talked to the parent of a prospective student sums up our work. "When a new boy comes to the ranch, the boys feel strange around the new boy, and the new boy feels strange around the boys at the ranch. And we tell him what is right and wrong at the ranch. Well, if he was to say a bad word, we would tell him it is wrong to say it. And he feels like everyone is watching him all the time, but we try to make him feel at home. After a while he settles down. He does not feel like a new boy. The way I felt when I first came to the ranch was shy and scared to talk to anyone, but then there are boys who are very different than I. They come and act like they have known us for years—like one boy, five minutes after his parents left him here he knew the boys better than I did, and I had been here for a week. Well, why don't you send your boy here and see how he acts, and he will be a new boy when he comes home."

Another little boy after an evening worship wrote a note to me in his crooked handwriting. "I want to be Jesus' boy." Then he drew a happy face.

The boys asked to have special classes at my home in the evening, to which I agreed, suggesting Wednesday night. "We need to know more about the Bible and what it teaches," one of the older boys said. "Could we meet here three times a week?"

The others chorused their approval, but I also had to consider the time I would need to prepare the lessons. Finally we compromised on two nights a week plus the Sabbath. Although attendance was strictly voluntary, all but three or four of the boys were there for each meeting. The boys had seen so many answered prayers that as one of them said, "I couldn't help but be a believer."

One evening during our meeting, Steve felt a real burden for the boys who hadn't come. "Dear Lord," he prayed, "those boys need to be here at our meeting. Won't You please put a touch in their hearts?" The Lord heard and answered that simple and sincere request. Before long two of those boys were coming.

Many of the boys learned to know Jesus in a personal way and were baptized in a little moun-

It's a Boys' World

tain stream near the school. As the young former "incorrigibles" started a new life, I was sure that here was one of those rewards that are beyond purchase.

Someone once said to me, "You couldn't pay me to do your work."

I told him, "No, I wouldn't do it *for pay*, either."

One of the boys asked, "When you were little, did they tell you Jesus was coming soon?"

"Yes," I told him, "they said Jesus was coming very soon."

"Well, aren't you a little disappointed He hasn't come yet?"

An interesting and profitable discussion followed. "I used to wish Jesus would come right away," Brian volunteered, "but I'm glad He didn't, 'cause I wasn't ready."

"Neither was I," the first boy continued. "I'm not sure if I am right now, but I'm a lot more ready since I came to the ranch than five years ago when I prayed that He'd come right away. Now I hope He comes *real* soon."

That makes it all worthwhile.

We've had more than our share of trials. Angela's death was the hardest thing we've ever had to bear. The schoolhouse fire, our loss of Ruthie, the threats of violence in Welcome Valley, and all the other problems we faced and continue to face, become bearable only when we realize . . .

"If we would hear the angels sing,

Or join the heavenly choir;
We first must trust the sweetest Name
Who rules o'er death and fire."